Taekwondo

The Unity of Body, Mind and Spirit

KOREA ESSENTIALS No. 13

Taekwondo: The Unity of Body, Mind and Spirit

First Published in 2013 by Seoul Selection
B1 Korean Publishers Association Bldg., 105-2 Sagan-dong, Jongno-gu, Seoul
110-190, Korea
Phone: (82-2) 734-9567
Fax: (82-2) 734-9562
Email: publisher@seoulselection.com
Website: www.seoulselection.com

ISBN: 978-89-97639-37-3 04080
ISBN: 978-89-91913-70-7 (set)
Printed in the Republic of Korea

Taekwondo

The Unity of Body, Mind and Spirit

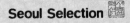

CONTENTS

Appendix
Information 113

Delving Deeper

INTRODUCTION

Hadi Saei became not only taekwondo's greatest Olympian, winning two golds and a bronze, but his nation's greatest Olympian. He returned to his native Iran a hero on three separate occasions. But as an athlete he decided not to cash in on his fame. Instead, he sold his medals to raise funds for the victims of the 2003 Iran earthquake and entered politics. Is it the sport that makes the man or the man that makes the sport? Saei, in setting out on an ethical journey beyond the realms of his sport, is not an anomalous figure in the history of taekwondo. And yet taekwondo is a sport that didn't even have an official name until 1955. In the days before codified rules, there was no protective gear and one-round matches simply persisted until a player was quelled. The journey from those early days of the rudimentary *gwan* (gymnasium) to the Olympic finals that utilize touch-sensitive electronic scoring chest protectors is the story of one national sport's unprecedented rise.

The post-World War II advancement of taekwondo has been rapid and global, yet there is a greater time frame in which it can be set. Going back millennia, taekwondo enthusiasts may find the roots of Korean native martial arts in the ancient bands of border warriors, who combined a love of unarmed combat with a love of common virtue and education. This book begins by touching on that past, and proceeds to look at taekwondo's relationship with Zen philosophy, the aesthetic significance of the *dobok*, taekwondo's uniform, and the system of belts.

But a concise survey of taekwondo must lend most of its space to what has happened since 1945, when Korea regained its independence in two halves. Freed from a foreign dictatorship that systematically smothered the boldest forms of Korean cultural expression, Korean martial arts reemerged like a tiger freed from a trap. The metaphor is a deliberate one, since the animal that once roamed the Korean Peninsula lends its name to several taekwondo groups, including a world-famous demonstration troupe and a martial arts-trained special ops force, formed at the height of the Korean War.

Modern taekwondo has thrust itself onto the world sports scene by way of an extensive government—propelled program at home and vigorous pioneering by its early masters abroad. Today, just about every major city on the globe boasts at least one *dojang* (gymnasium).

A look at taekwondo in the *dojang* itself will explore technical aspects, from the roundhouse kick to the difference between the ITF (International Taekwondo Federation) and WTF (World Taekwondo Federation), before concluding with a glimpse into taekwondo's future. All along the way, we will be delving deeper into taekwondo with a look at the events, places, and people who make this martial art the one that dominates all others.

"Taekwondo is a great gift that Korea has given to the world."

- George Vitale
8th-degree black belt, American taekwondo senior master

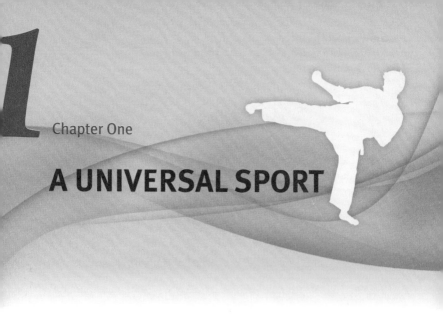

Chapter One

A UNIVERSAL SPORT

In recent decades, Korea has raised its global sporting profile with success in numerous world competitive events. In golf, where as of 2013 Korean women held four out of the top ten ranking positions; in soccer, where the national side reached the semifinals of the World Cup Korea co-hosted in 2002; and with repeated Olympic golds in archery and wrestling, amongst others, Korea can justifiably add sport to electronics, automotive manufacturing, scientific research and even pop music in its portfolio of achievements in the modern world. Korea's success in archery and wrestling are rooted in the country's indigenous versions of the sports, practiced over millennia. But their expression is achieved in an internationally codified form of the sports that Korean competitors must adapt to as an agreed-upon standard. So if you were to ask the average international sports fan which sport they most closely identify with Korea, he or she would say none of the above. The answer would be taekwondo. And today, eighty million people around the world practice the Korean martial art.

The word taekwondo instantly conjures up the image of men and women dressed in *dobok*, the taekwondo uniform, belt tail hanging down from its sides, wearing, if in contest, protective head and body gear as they deploy one of dozens of endlessly drilled blocks, kicks, and punches on the padded surface of a *dojang*. By 1989 taekwondo, a sport whose first international federation, the ITF, wasn't founded until 1966, was the most popular martial art in the world. Just how did this ancient folk method of unarmed self-defense rise in that brief span of decades to become a competitive event in the Pan-American, Asian, and African Games, before full acceptance as an official Olympic sport at Sydney in 2000?

Taekwondo quarterfinal match in 2012 London Summer Olympics

The answer is to be found in the breadth of taekwondo's appeal. Like kimchi or ginseng, taekwondo is synonymous with Korea. Specific features of Korea's culture and history gave birth to taekwondo and determined its evolution: the country's wildlife, clothing, climate, forests and mountains. Its religious and cultural beliefs are all entwined in the practice and ethics of taekwondo. To learn taekwondo is to immerse oneself in a mental approach to physical combat deriving from a particular place. However, the rapid spread and popular appeal of taekwondo across every continent suggests that the art incorporates characteristics that transcend the local and national. Taekwondo has been accepted and disseminated by third-party adherents, independent of Koreans themselves, and has made its own contribution to world culture in the way that, say, Korean ceramics have done. It holds universal appeal.

Identifying a single element that gives taekwondo its universal appeal is as elusive as trying to identify a single element of any other artistic or cultural product that has achieved world renown. But the general observer might note how taekwondo's harmonistic eastern ethos is conjoined with a well-defined systematization of sporting rules and principles to form a pastime open to all, an all-inclusive form of activity, expression, hobby, and play.

Taekwondo combines ancient elements of ritual etiquette with physical exercise. It can be practiced alone or in a room with a hundred fellow players. It can be practiced in a winter camp deep in the *Jirisan* mountain or in the humid air of a Seoul rooftop in July. And this flexibility can and has been transferred to any environment in the world: Uganda, Brunei, Afghanistan, Siberia—all have *dojang*. Taekwondo's reuniting of man with his environment is not the only abiding, atavistic part of its appeal. It also engages as a

permanent bastion of respect in a modern world which, in many parts, has experienced a dissolution of the old foundations of authority. A practitioner of taekwondo cannot be respected solely through a display of technically advanced aggression. This martial art stresses the ritual of processes in the same way as other touchstones of the traditional do, such as the Korean tea at the ceremony. Practitioners of taekwondo, be they advanced combatants official match level or part time dilettantes, can all appreciate this martial arts depth.

AN EXCITING SPORT—BASIC RULES OF TAEKWONDO

Athens, 2004. The Olympic Taekwondo Hall of the Faliron Olympic Complex. The capacity 8,000-strong crowd is as on edge as the athletes adjusting their head gear for the final time before they enter the 10m × 10m ring. They approach, face each other, and pause briefly before bowing from the waist. "Start!" shouts the referee,who urges them to fight with a swift wave of his hand. Hadi Saei of Iran is impatient, bouncing forward on his heels, itching to strike first, whilst Song Myeong-seob, the young South Korean, checks his defensive position.

Hadi Saei can wait no longer, and shuffles rapidly forward to launch a front kick at Song's face. He misses, slips, and falls. It is a bad start. Saei jumps up and Song pursues him to the middle of the floor, the referee standing between the two. A full 30 seconds pass as they cagily face off, neither wishing to repeat Saei's early mistake.

Saei attacks again. He connects with a long front kick, but as the scorer clocks up the Iranian's point, Song responds with a naraechagi double-turn pivot kick. The naraechagi has been kinematically analyzed in the Korean Journal of Physical Education to take, on average, 0.88 seconds, 53.4 percent of that time used up in preparation moves, which were all but invisible behind the Iranian's front kick. The time between attack and defense is so short, so adept are the world's premier taekwondo athletes, that they seem to attack simultaneously. The judges face a hard task separating the two.

It remains 1:1 for twenty seconds, a period in which Saei has decided that somehow, in the milliseconds between attack and defense, between thought and action, he has gained the upper hand in the psychological battle. He once again launches the first attack. But once again, before his foot can properly connect, Song responds, and the exchange raises the score to 2:2. Round one ends with the men exchanging almost imperceptible bows.

Two fighters. Three two-minute rounds. One point for an attack to the body protector. Three points for a kick to the head. Foot techniques only allowed using the parts of the foot below the ankle. Fist techniques, in competitive WTF competition, must utilize a closed hand. Appeals, interruptions. Points awarded when permitted techniques deliver full force, abrupt displacement, and trembling shock to the legal scoring areas of the body. Disagreement between judges resolved with majority electronic voting. Warnings, point deductions. Deduction of four points entails an automatic loss. Don't hit an opponent below the waist. Never hit an opponent who is on the ground. If it is a draw after three rounds, a golden point round is played. Thousands of knowledgeable supporters. Tens of millions of players. This is Olympic taekwondo. These are the rules. But this is not the final. This is the semifinal of the men's under 68kg competition, and an epically tight first round sets the stage for one of the great Olympic taekwondo battles.

The match ends all square, nine points each after the third round. But Saei progresses to the final when a penalty point is deducted from Song, whose appeals prove futile. Saei takes the gold against Taiwan's Huang Chih-Hsiung. Song, eight years his opponent's junior, goes on to clinch bronze in the third-place match.

2008 Beijing Summer Olympics

Taekwondo may be described as an unarmed, hard, and linear style of martial arts combat, characterized by a unique emphasis on foot skills. The sparring "taekwondoist" is required to follow a dynamic adjustment of poses, throwing strikes from a mobile stance. Taekwondo players employ punches, takedowns, kicks, blocks, open-handed strikes, throws, joint locks, grabbing techniques, and pressure point manipulation to overcome an opponent. It is a martial art that has developed into its modern form under the premise that the legs have a greater reach and power than the arms. Taekwondo's point of contradistinction with other martial arts is therefore its emphasis on rapid and powerful kicking techniques. There is less focus on the redirection of force. Pose-forming patterns in taekwondo are called *poomsae*, and the utilization of the correct pose will serve to enable the correct block or cracking-down maneuver when striking the opponent, thus delivering greater destructive power. Practitioners graduate through a system of colored belts before they attain master status. The ceiling of official advancement is 9th *dan* black belt, or grandmaster status, a rarely conferred honor achieved by a small company of the most illustrious and esteemed figures in taekwondo's history. Achieving it requires a lifetime's

dedication to a martial art that venerates dedication and identifies itself martial arts of the distant past.

THE ROOT OF KOREA'S MARTIAL ARTS

On June 1, 1983, Shin Han-seung was unveiled as Korea's first cultural human asset. The appellation is applied only to an individual in whom the government believes resides unique knowledge and skill in a particular aspect of traditional Korean culture. That the first person upon whom the title was bestowed was an adept of the ancient Korean martial art of *taekkyeon* illustrates the importance attached to native combat forms of self-defense in Korea. Shin was recognized as the person who formally systematized *taekkyeon*, an art which lives on not just as an independent art of itself but as one of several root progenitors of taekwondo.

Written historical records are sparse and provide little documented information regarding the details of Korea's indigenous martial arts defense systems. But *taekkyeon* can be dated back at least as far as the Goguryeo Kingdom (37BC–AD668), one of the peninsula's historical forerunners to the modern Korean nation. *Taekkyeon*'s early development has to be viewed in the context of Goguryeo's fluctuating borders with modern day China, into which Goguryeo extended over some considerable distance. These borders changed hands frequently, giving rise to a natural exchange of military and martial techniques, which included unarmed combat.

TAEKWONDO IN AFGHANISTAN

Afghanistan has experienced decades of civil and regional wars. Ordinary life, for many, has become a complicated organizational matter set against a backdrop of safety and security concerns. Added to that are often fiercely implemented cultural strictures that militate against the importation of new ideas and practices. Remarkably, then, Afghans have shown such enthusiasm for taekwondo, it has survived during one of the most trying periods in the country's history to become a thriving and well recognized sport.

The Afghan Taekwondo Federation (ATF) was founded by two brothers, Master M. Yousuf Dildar and Master Usman Didldar, in 1990, and was officially recognized by the WTF in 1993. The ATF is not merely a nominal "paper" organization, having dispatched teams to participate in the 1994 Asian Games and the 2002 Asian Taekwondo Championships in Aman, Jordan. The journey of the Dildar brothers is emblematic of the journey of taekwondo around the world.

The two began practicing taekwondo in 1988, and by 1992, Usman was elected secretary general of the Afghan Taewkondo Federation. He left for the United Kingdom in 1993 and, after receiving his 4th *dan*, established the London Taekwondo Academy, opening a second branch soon thereafter. Usman has become a national referee, and in July 2000, participated in the 3rd Foreign Instructors Training Course at the Kukkiwon in Seoul.

His brother Yousuf has promoted more than a thousand Afghan taekwondo

The situation in the region necessitated amongst the ancient Koreans a ready proficiency in fighting skills, and a recognized, teachable martial art for national defense. *Taekkyeon* filled this need, and those records which reference its role, such as *Goryeosa* (*History of Goryeo*), *Sejongsillok jiriji* (*Cultural Geography in the Veritable Records of King Sejong*), *Jaemulbo* (*Dictionary of Names of Things in the Universe*), *Joseon Sanggosa* (*Early History of*

practitioners to black belt, traveling to most provinces of that vast country in the process. By 1995, he had opened thirty branches of schools over the border in Pakistan, before taking the first Afghanistan taekwondo team to an overseas event at the Japan Asian Games. He is involved in taekwondo academies in the UK, Holland, and Iran.

The payoff of the Dildar brothers' endeavors in the name of Afghani taekwondo has been globally tangible. Rohullah Nikpai took bronze in the men's taekwondo 58kg at the 2008 Beijing Olimpics, becoming the first Afghani to win a Summer Olympics medal. He repeated the feat in the 68 kg taekwondo event in London four years later. Elsewhere, Nesar Ahmad Bahave, after winning a silver and bronze in the 2006 Asian Games, won two silvers in the Beijing 2007 World Taekwondo Championships. Such consistent achievements suggest the Dildar brothers have sown the seeds of taekwondo deeply in Afghani sporting culture, and that we have not heard the last of their country at international events.

Korea), *Donggukyeojiseungnam* (*Augmented Survey of the Geography of Korea*), all indicate that *taekkyeon* was promoted by the Korean proto-state. Cave and tomb murals of the period include scenes of men apparently engaged in *taekkyeon* contests.

Koreans of the Goguryeo period had succeeded in ruling over a large stretch of land, in part, through advanced equestrian and archery skills. *Taekkyeon* formed the third element of this fighting triumvirate. In *taekkyeon* can be found precursors of the unique footwork movements of taekwondo to come, and lineage with the modern day sport's varied kicking techniques. The *seonbae* ("a man of virtue who never retreats from a fight") were a group-dwelling warrior corps trained in early Korean martial arts. *Taekkyeon* was a vitalizing element amongst Goguryeo Koreans, but it did not end with the kingdom. The martial art has since been practiced in every era of Korean history, though with varying degrees of official enthusiasm.

This painting shows Koreans enjoying themselves as they watch *taekkyeon* and *ssireum*, two martial arts that are original to Korea.
A Joyful Scene (大快圖), Joseon Dynasty, 18th–19th Century, National Museum of Korea

Geumgang *makgi* (blocks) © kukkiwon

Geumgangyeoksasang Statues
(a guardian of a temple gate),
Seokguram Grotto

The *Hwarang* of the Silla Empire (668–935) are cited as the organized inspiration for modern taekwondo's physical and aesthetic principles. The *Hwarang* was a youth corps of military adepts that helped unify Korea under Silla rule. The corps was formed at a time when the integrity of the peninsula was under threat from Japanese pirates, and the former resolve of Goguryeo had abated. *Hwarangdo* literally means the "way of flowering manhood," and its young initiates were fiercely dedicated to systematically disseminating their martial belief system. But as implied in their somewhat nebulous title, the *Hwarang*'s approach to defending the Silla Empire was not defined by purely physical methods. Schools were established in numerous provinces where young men studied history, Confucian philosophy, ethics, Buddhist morality, and military tactics, all in addition to *taekkyeon* and the fundamentals of physical combat. In taekwondo's early days of the 1950s, black belts were required to memorize the *Hwarang*'s five venerable rules: loyalty to the king, filial love toward one's parents,

SSIREUM

Among the better known of traditional individual sports in Korea are *ssireum*, the Korean cousin of Western wrestling, and *subak*, a prototype of taekwondo.The oldest recorded form of *ssireum* can be seen on the mural in the Gakjeochong Tomb dating back to the 5th–6th century Goguryeo. Located in Tungkou, in parts of China once known as Manchuria, this ancient tomb has a large painting of a *ssireum* contest on the east wall of the burial chamber.

The painting shows two grappling men, clad in loincloths. Their hands are gripping each other's loincloth and their feet are planted firmly in the ground. One of them casts his eyes downward, his shoulder muscles taut and tensed, while the other's face is upturned, his mouth slightly agape as if short of breath.

Contrasting with the athletic poses of these two strong men, a patriarch with flowing white beard leans on his cane and spectates. It appears that the old man is refereeing the match.

The Annals of Korea has this to say: "Young people play *ssireum* on Mt. Namsan or behind Sinmumun Gate of Mt. Bugaksan. The rule is for two men to sit on their knees face to face, knees touching each other's. Each grabs the other by the belt with his right hand and the thigh with his left hand. They push themselves up together to the standing position and grapple until one forces the other down to defeat. *Ssireum* involves a number of techniques such as hooking in the leg, hooking out the leg, and lifting. Chinese call it Goryeogi, or the Goryeo sport."

This description of *ssireum* from the 19th century evokes the impression from the 5th–6th century Goguryeo tomb painting, demonstrating that the ancient sport was passed down without much alteration in its style for over a thousand years. Indeed, *ssireum* and *subak* were not totally separated from each other until as recently as the mid-17th century.

There is no doubt, however, that courage was nurtured among combat sports from the distant past.

*Album of Genre Painting by Danwon,
Joseon Dynasty, 18th Century, Treasure
No.527, National Museum of Korea*

A *takkyeon* class

fidelity in friendship, bravery in battle, and no wanton killing or unnecessary violence. The *Hwarang* viewed man's advanced knowledge of a fighting system as essentially naked if it lacked an underpinning of ethical principles. In the provinces, the *Hwarang* met a people receptive to the idea of such a national education, and through *taekkyeon* and other indigenous self defense combat forms, they established and "nationalized" martial arts in Korea that were already centuries old.

Taekkyeon was not taught solely for the purpose of protecting the integrity of tribal lands. Throughout the centuries, there were organized games at which *taekkyeon*—also known as or very similar to the Korean indigenous martial art of *subak*—featured as a regular and popular contest spectacle. The proselytizing mindset that would one day achieve the promotion of taekwondo to a full Olympic sport was seeded by the *Hwarang* and this early spirit of competition.

MUYEDOBOTONGJI

Muyedobotongji, a comprehensive illustrated manual of Korean martial arts published during the Joseon Dynasty (1392–1910), is an especially significant record in that it includes not only information about Korean martial arts but also describes how the martial arts and fighting techniques of other countries came to be known in Korea. It served to expand the application of martial arts using the bow and the sword for military purposes rather than personal endeavors.

Muyedobotongji was commissioned by King Jeongjo (r. 1776–1800) and published in four volumes in 1790, the 14th year of Jeongjo's reign. It was compiled by Yi Deok-mu (1741–1793) and Bak Je-ga (1750–1805) based on the state of military affairs at the time. There is an additional volume in which the original Chinese characters are presented in the Korean script, Hangeul.

The motivation for this major publication was related to the foreign invasions of Korea during the Joseon Dynasty, in particular the Japanese

(left, right) Rreenactments of traditional martial arts based on *Muyedobotongji*

invasions led by the warlord Toyotomi Hideyoshi and the Byeongja Horan, an offensive by Qing China. These invasions shattered the peace of the first 200 years of the Joseon Dynasty, thus arousing in the king and commoners alike the need to revive Korea's martial arts.

As previously mentioned, *Muyedobotongji* explains how elements of Chinese and Japanese martial arts were incorporated into Korean martial arts. In particular, the recording of Japanese swordsmanship, or waegeom, demonstrates the importance that Koreans placed on knowing their enemies well to devise defensive countermeasures.

The book is divided into 24 chapters, dealing with a variety of martial art forms. The first volume is devoted to spear fighting, with six chapters on different techniques. The second covers sword fighting, with two chapters on traditional Korean techniques and one on Japanese swordsmanship. The third contains eight chapters describing various types of sword fighting, while the fourth is dedicated to six martial arts including the "fist method," gwonbeop, and various horse-mounted martial arts. At the end of the book is an appendix providing detailed illustrations of the clothing worn in four martial arts. It is thus a valuable reference for the study of ancient clothing.

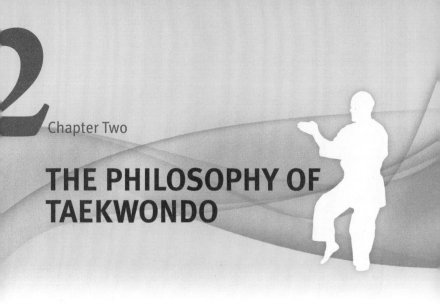

Chapter Two

THE PHILOSOPHY OF TAEKWONDO

It is no an overstatement to say taekwondo is one of the most significant cultural vehicles through which Koreans seek to globalize their culture. Although much success has been attained in popularizing taekwondo and developing it as a competitive sport, not much has been done to promote its philosophical aspects. Taekwondo is a martial art underpinned by philosophical and aesthetic worldviews, operating in a realm of expanded "human activity."

WHITE OUTFIT AND BELTS

Taekwondo is practiced wearing a white jacket and trousers, with a belt worn around the waist. White was the color of Korean clothing in ancient times, and Koreans were sometimes called the "white-clad" people. These three items serve to represent the three "ultimates" in East Asian thought: Heaven, Earth and Man, collectively referred to as *ban* or *hanbeol*. The taekwondo outfit, called *dobok*, is similar in broad aspects of design with the traditional Korean costume *hanbok*.

Among the basic forms of Korean attire, the jacket (*jeogori*) is worn by both men and women. The men's jacket comes down to the buttocks in the back, has long sleeves, and is marked by lines defining the lapels, front, and sleeve openings. The jacket is brought together and tied like a caftan. In ancient times, the front was fastened with either the left or right side underneath until it was determined—as seen in paintings of figures on the walls of Goguryeo tombs—that the right side should overlap the left around the sixth century. The trousers, an essential garment of northern nomadic people, have been worn since before the Three Kingdoms period. References to the *Buyeo* people in the "Tong-i-zhuan"

section of the Chinese Sangua-zhi historical records note, "The *Buyeo* people wore trousers of white cloth and straw shoes." The *dobok* white color is meant to concord with indigenous Korean philosophy. Since the essence of the universe and the source of all things are white, we are all essentially derived from one (*han*, or *hana*). *Han*, which also means white, symbolizes the essence of the universe.

The belt completes the taekwondo uniform. Belts imprinted with a horse insignia recovered from Bronze Age historical sites suggest that the belt originated as part of a tribal outfit. During Goguryeo times, the aristocracy wore wide belts made of hemp or silk, whereas commoners

wore those of a narrow width and the lower class used braided rope to secure their trousers. During the mid-Joseon period, belts were usually worn with outer garments such as overcoats. Today, there are taekwondo belts of many colors. Tying the belt over the jacket highlights the beauty of a curved line as the loose end of the belt sways freely during a match. When taken off, it is straight; when worn on the waist, circular; and when tied, its ends curve. In addition to the aesthetics of a curved line, the belt also can be seen as an expression of the Five Elements. That is to say, it represents the primal Supreme Ultimate, with the area above the waist being yang and that below yin.

There is a symbolic logic to the

Goguryeo Costume

The *dobok* white color is meant to concord with indigenous Korean philosophy.

development of belt colors, from white to black, which serves as an extended metaphor through a daily life cycle. The new student has no knowledge of taekwondo, and white symbolizes the purity of an initiate, the stage of pre-emergence. The initiate's first point of progression will then be to acquire a yellow belt. He or she is, like the rising sun, starting out on a journey which will end and begin again with the black of night. Once the seed of knowledge has been planted and basic taekwondo techniques begin to grow, the belt color will, upon passing the next exam, change to green, the color of an emerging plant. As growth reaches upwards, it is reflected in the blue of the sky, the next belt color. The brown belt that follows symbolizes that the student has reached a position of stability, just as a growing plant is rooted in soil. Red, the color of blood, life's essential flowing force, reflects the setting sun before black, the color created when all others have been absorbed into an object, takes control.

UNDERSTANDING TAEKWONDO'S PHILOSOPHY

Kim Yeong-seon, a taekwondo instructor at Yonsei University in Seoul, says, "The philosophy of taekwondo is not limited to an investigation of essence and fundamental principles. It is the living philosophy of taekwondo practitioners." In other words, without the proper consciousness, actions will be distorted. Anyone but a committed pacifist would argue that when confronted with potential violence, it is natural to defend oneself. The matter of what action one should take in response to such circumstances is an important question. In such situations, one is often compelled to act dictated by the relevant circumstances. A person who has devoted himself to training for the purpose of improving the effectiveness of his or her actions will have an improved ability to react.

A deeper look into the mental elements of taekwondo shows a

clear relationship with Zen thought. Zen consistently recognizes the significance of human action itself, while stressing the flow from one movement to another. Taekwondo, like Zen, rejects the need to pause within a situation for reflection, considering this an effete distraction.

The goal of Zen practitioners is to attain a state of non-self. When this is achieved, the duality of self and opponent as well as that between consciousness and action can be overcome. In such a state, there is only oneself, as one becomes an integral part of the overall situation. The person can discern the situation as it is. For example, when in a match, if a competitor focuses exclusively on a certain movement of the opponent, he or she will tend to lose concentration of the situation as a whole. On the other hand, if he or she strives to realize self-consciousness, he or she can better react to a movement by the opponent. Without awareness, one can intuitively sense a movement within the sphere of action, so always being prepared to fend off one's opponent.

Among taekwondo practitioners, only those who genuinely learn the finer points of the art will realize its philosophical essence. Those who practice taekwondo or another martial art as a hobby during their spare time, for exercise or as a means of self-defense will gain a certain level of benefit through such training; but taekwondo offers a mental fulfillment that goes far beyond its physical nature. Such advanced learning cannot be achieved by practicing taekwondo alone. A proper orientation can be acquired only by learning from a skilled teacher while adhering to the traditions and rules of the training center, under the guiding influence of one's fellow senior and junior members. Moreover, it is possible to obtain profound wisdom about life from an ancient value system and an understanding of the unique philosophy of taekwondo. Such a philosophy is easier to understand than to carry out in daily life, but possible after years of practice.

AESTHETICS OF TAEKWONDO

The aesthetics of taekwondo can be divided into the passive and dynamic aspects. The passive aesthetics of taekwondo are apparent in the static and unmoving tranquility of its mental training as expressed in meditation and the way mind and body become one through this internal contemplation of the activities of external training. The dynamic aesthetics are seen in the vitality and strength of movement during training itself.

Passive Aesthetics

A strong emphasis is on mental training in taekwondo. In the quiet beauty of the forms and movements themselves, a greater value and meaning can be found. The key to the forms and movements of taekwondo is that the mind and body should move together, not only the visible physical movements but also control of the emotions and breath that flow from the mind. Through this control, the mind becomes clear while the flowing movement of the body is enhanced. When the body and mind move together, movement that is neither moving nor stationary can be understood. It is an extremely calm and flowing state of mind in which consciousness of the movements themselves disappears.

The forms and movements of taekwondo are, therefore, not merely the flow and movement of the body but also include the internal movement of the Tao, that rarefied principle of the universe. Tao attained from taekwondo training is Tao realized through the world of the subconscious. Only when this subconscious Tao can be expressed through the body can the activity of the practitioner be at one with nature and the universe; the practitioner's movement has become an expression of ultimate beauty and the zenith of the art. This is more than an external expression of aesthetics. It is a mental pursuit of tranquility that vividly demonstrates the uniquely intellectual character of taekwondo. The time and place in which the performance occurs create a world free from common concerns and anxieties, and this reverent state of mind is the noble and lofty goal of taekwondo. The art's passive aesthetics are not the beauty of non-moving states themselves but the stillness inherent in taekwondo movements; a stillness within which the practitioner and the wondrous natural world are visibly joined together.

To understand the fundamental philosophy and ideology of taekwondo, one must learn the theoretical principles upon which its movements are based. The art is a practical application of these principles as expressed in the *taegeuk*, the yin and yang symbol, representing the negative and positive aspects of universal life. Consequently, the lines of movement are a complete and practical expression of the principles of the yin-yang lines of the eight trigrams: offense and defense, retreat and advance, gentleness and strength, and fast and slow.

During training, the body's extension and retraction, breathing rate, strength and weakness must all be controlled. The lines of movement in the forms and activities of taekwondo are expressions of the yin-yang lines of the eight trigrams, each representing a fundamental principle of the universe. As such, breathing, the feel of a movement, and the movement's speed are performed with a high degree of control, so that each aspect is an application of the cosmology of the *taegeuk*.

The philosophical foundation of the forms and movements of

taekwondo is thus established in this manner. The many hours of repetitive kicking, striking, and blocking willingly undertaken by the practitioner are not simply mindless repetitions; they are intended to reinforce the importance and meaning of postures, positioning of the feet and hands, direction, and control of breathing and muscles.

During periods of training, when in the ready position or when the muscles are relaxed, the practitioner is waiting for just the right moment, when all of the body's energy is concentrated on one point for an attack. This type of repetitive training can be viewed as a non-aggressive practice, with mental concentration being a form of meditative discipline.

Meditation is pursued to realize liberation. At this stage, it becomes possible to understand the basic principles of worldly matters and thus a profound understanding and anticipation of special movements is possible as well. An experienced professional tennis player seeks to anticipate the direction from which a ball will be returned, and then he or she prepares for the situation. In taekwondo, mental concentration is even more important. Taekwondo training is conducted in a systematic and organized manner, the tangible expression of which is manifested in the forms and movements that make up the essence of the art. In this way, practicing the forms and movements of the art makes the human impulses and instincts sublime.

This process of sublimation is the mental state of transcendence, a state of absence. In this state, the practitioner is unaware of the enemy in front, the emotions associated with victory and defeat, bravery and fear, negative thoughts, and desires such as revenge and ambition. All should be absent from the mind. Ultimately, taekwondo becomes a way of controlling the manner in which one expresses oneself and one's aggression, a highly effective means of controlling violent tendencies.

TAEKWONDO AND BALLET

The basic physical requirements for taekwondo and ballet are good flexibility and core strength. Ava May Llewellyn has both in abundance. She started dancing when she was two years old and began taekwondo lessons at the precocious age of four. The young student trained in ballet at the Dance Station and attended taekwondo lessons at the North Bristol Taekwondo School. The study of one failed to inhibit or slow progress in the other, and she eventually became the first person with a martial art black belt to secure a place at England's prestigious Royal Ballet School in London, beating out 1,000 applicants around the world competing for the available 24 spots.

That the first black belt martial artist to study at the Royal Ballet School is a taekwondoist would not come as a surprise to Grandmaster Jhoon Rhee. Rhee is commonly known as the "father of American Taekwondo" for his proselytizing work spreading the sport in the United States. He is also the only Korean American named amongst the 203 most recognized immigrants to the country by the Immigration and Naturalization Service. In the 1970s, Rhee formulated what he called "martial ballet." Rooted in his deep knowledge of taekwondo, He sought to syncopate the thrusting motions and arcing movements of taekwondo with such pieces as Beethoven's Fifth Symphony. The moves displayed during the performance concord with the drama and tone of the melody to reorient traditional martial art in a multigenre form, transcending its prime physical purpose of self-defense.

Crossover between the two genres is not theoretically surprising. There is an obvious relationship between the complicated aerial kicks of taekwondo and the long balance and reach demanded by ballet. That taekwondo has proven itself an adaptive and amorphous sport suggests that Llewellyn has not just the talent and dedication necessary to augment Rhee's pioneering work, but to create something entirely new.

Dynamic Aesthetics

As with dance, which is expressed through the body's movements, so too taekwondo expresses its spirit and ideology through physical movements. The principles of dance and taekwondo have much in common. The forms and movements at the heart of taekwondo are also considered to be similar to traditional Korean dance and music. Taekwondo movements rely on flexibility and precision. This is especially true when a taekwondo practitioner raises his foot up above his head or attempts a highly technical kick, such as the flying reverse spinning kick, which can be used simultaneously for attack and defense. In ballet, with its elevated kicks, turns, jumps, and soft landings, and in forms of dance that use the entire body, can be seen the parallels between taekwondo and dance. As with dance and other performing arts, taekwondo includes distinctive artistic elements.

Taekwondo is an art based on movements. At the core of all of its movements is the distinctive curved line of traditional Korean aesthetics. The movements and forms of taekwondo feature the beautiful curved lines revered in Korean tradition, and their essence is the basic form of traditional Korean dance. Among the curved lines integrated in taekwondo movements, the themes of tranquility, gravity, and movement are the most prominent. Amid the tranquility of taekwondo movements, there is a profound expression of the universal energy *gi*, which gathers within the body, while through movement, energy and tranquility are maintained in equilibrium. The essence of the themes of tranquility, gravity, and action is reflected in each step and hand movement of taekwondo.

Taekwondo movements are forms that result from a dynamic and skillful engagement with the art, and it is within a structured framework that the practitioner replicates the forms and movements of the art. Repetition is an expression of one element of training. It embodies the goals of the art, and is a period of adjustment that continues until the beauty of the art can be refined. Only when the harmony and artistic grace of the movements are united through the process of repetitive training can the true elegance of taekwondo be achieved. In training, all movements are expressions of the essential nature of the art, with the basic principles of these movements being strength, precision, and speed. In these movements, each joint is used with the utmost vigor and precision.

The symbolic meaning of the structure of the forms and movements of taekwondo can be seen as an expression of the concept of an internal world. The forms and movements of the art in the external world can be seen as symbols of existence. The artistic elements of the discipline of taekwondo, those well-honed movements of the art that combine elegance and subtlety, expressed through bodily movements, create instances of beauty and a tangible realization of these outward expressions of beauty.

PRESIDENTIAL TAEKWONDOISTS

US President Barack Obama and former Korean President Lee Myung-bak

It is 1987. Dressed in a full *dobok*, jacket tied together with an honorary black belt, his formal neck tie peeking out from under his uniform Bill Clinton, then governor of Arkansas, addresses the room from a microphoned podium. He looks slightly less comfortable than usual. The man who will be sworn in to office as 39th president of the United States within five years is flanked by Master Hu Lee, president of the American Taekwondo Association (ATA). Clinton is here to talk about the American Grand National Taekwondo Contest, to be held in Little Rock, Arkansas, over Memorial Day weekend and featuring over three thousand competitors. Up to that date, it will be the largest martial arts event of one style in history. What started in 1976 as a closed national tournament has grown to be an international spectacular of competitive taekwondo.

After the politician has finished speaking, Master Hu gives the future president a one-minute taekwondo crash course. Governor Clinton is taught how to stand and correctly address a board, and Master Hu then invites him to smash it with a single strike of his left forearm. It sparked interest in taekwondo and prompted Clinton take up the martial art more seriously.

Bill Clinton is not the only US president to have been a skilled taekwondoist. Barack Obama practiced taekwondo for a number of years with an American master in Chicago, while he served in the Illinois state senate. President Obama advanced to green belt, and demonstrated his punch stance to photographers in Seoul when he made his first visit to Korea in 2009. Korean President Lee Myung-bak presented Obama with an honorary black belt as a memento of his stay.

Chapter Three

A MODERN HISTORY

THE FIRST GWAN

In March 1945, US troops arrived in the southern port city of Busan while Soviet forces entered the north. For the Korean people, it was the beginning of liberation from Japanese annexation and colonization; it also marked a de facto division of the peninsula. For indigenous martial arts, the end of the Second World War was to herald the commencement of a rapid and diverse flowering. Sports that had been suppressed by the occupiers now found official training outlets in the first five *gwan*. The *gwan* were the major martial arts schools that opened in the years immediately after Korea regained its independence.

The five original *gwan* were founded by individuals who were to have a seminal influence on the development of modern taekwondo. In most cases, they were multi-skilled martial artists, equipped with a grounding in the arts of at least one other country, usually China or Japan, as well as mastery of Korean *taekkyeon* or *subak*. The speed with which the five prosaically named *gwan* were established is telling, and suggests an inevitability to the process by which a fully-formed modern Korean martial art would evolve.

Cheongdogwan was opened in 1944 by Lee Won-kuk. "The School of the Blue Wave" soon grew in renown, thanks in no small part to the efforts of its founder, an adept of *taekkyeon* who had studied karate in Okinawa and kung fu in Henan. In the same year, Songmugwan ('The School of the Pine Tree') was opened by Ro Byung-jik. Ro's son, Hee-sang, was also to become an important figure in the history of taekwondo, going on to win numerous championships and becoming a renowned military instructor.

Mudeokgwan's founder, Hwang Gi, embodies the cross fertilization of martial arts characteristic of modern taekwondo's

Cheongdogwan in Pohang 1961 (source: Korea Taekwondo Association, www.koreataekwondo.org)

The First of Nine *Gwan*

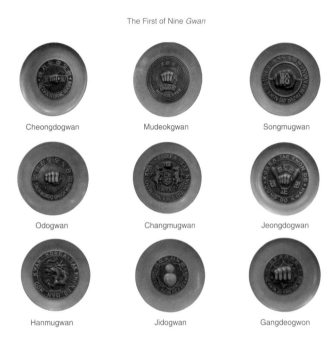

Cheongdogwan	Mudeokgwan	Songmugwan
Odogwan	Changmugwan	Jeongdogwan
Hanmugwan	Jidogwan	Gangdeogwon

inception, as well as the personal rivalries that typified its development until organizational unification in later years. Hwang is said to have studied under Lee Won-kuk at Cheongdogwan, something Hwang himself denied, claiming another Korean martial arts master, Yang Kuk-jin, as his teacher. Hwang had been a student of *taekkyeon*, tai chi, kung fu, and karate, and thus his eventual school, 'The School of Martial Virtue', bore a generalized designation. After faltering starts in his attempts to establish a school, Gi's Mudeokgwan rose to such a level of respected prominence that at one point, it could claim an influential hand in the martial arts style of three quarters of Korea's practitioners.

The *Gwonbeop dojang* ('The School of the Fist Method')

eventually changed its name to Changmugwan, under the direction of star student Lee Nam-suk. Lee took on the mantle of running the school after its founder Yoon Byong-in went missing during the Korean War. Yoon had studied kung fu under a Mongolian instructor in Manchuria, the region of north-eastern China to which a million Koreans had coercively migrated under Japanese occupation. Later on, while studying karate at a Japanese university, Yoon's special blend of self-defense techniques became apparent to students and teachers, who requested that he teach them everything he had learned.

The fifth of the original five *gwan* was Yeonmugwan, which was opened in March 1946. Its founder, Jeon Sang-seop, was close to Yoon Byong-in, the two having traveled to Manchuria to train together. Jeon's itinerant, peer-influenced development belies the fact that the school he founded had previously been the Japanese Judo School in Korea. Renaming implied a change in style at a time when ancient indigenous martial arts in Korea were experiencing a resurgence. A sad coincidence saw Jeon, like his close friend Yoon,

disappear during the Korean War. But the school survived and another change of name, to Jidogwan, brought about a new emphasis and further evolution of indigenous Korean martial arts.

In the tumult of these early post-liberation years, it could not yet be said that a competitive martial art called taekwondo existed. The profusion of appellations that the five *gwan* used to describe what they practiced, however, demonstrated that Korean martial artists focused on hand use in martial arts techniques. Cheongdogwan, for example, called its style "the way of the

A training manual of *Gwonbeop* (1955)

Chinese hand," while Yeonmugwan employed "the way of the empty hand." The foot, for now, was relegated to a supporting role. Clearly, the styles in Korean martial arts would not be harmonized without the influence of one or more predominant martial artists.

THE GENERAL

There are innumerable figures key to the mid-twentieth century beginnings of modern taekwondo. Few, however, can challenge the centrality of Choi Hong-hi in the sport's development. Choi, otherwise known as the father of taekwondo, was born on November 9, 1918, in Hwadae, a rugged area, in what is now North Korea. His frail physique as a boy contrasted with his willful streak of combativeness. A sickly nature did not prevent him from agitating the occupying Japanese, an act of youthful bravery that resulted in his expulsion from school. His worried father dispatched Choi to study calligraphy under a tutor, Han Il-dong, who happened to be a master of *taekkyeon*. Han set his frail student to work in an effort to match the boy's body to his will. A true but apocryphal sounding story involves the precocious Choi stepping up his *taekkyeon* training after getting involved in a dispute with a local giant of a Korean wrestler.

In 1937, Choi was sent to continue his studies in Japan, culminating in a second-degree black belt in karate while studying at university in Tokyo. Upon his return to Korea in 1942, and despite his best efforts to avoid being conscripted, Choi was forced to enlist in basic training in the Japanese army. Soon after, while serving in Pyongyang, he was implicated in the independence movement and imprisoned on charges of treason. Symbolically, however, Choi was to continue protesting from his cell, where he relentlessly practiced *taekkyeon* and other martial arts skills he had picked up in Japan. His routine caught the eye not just of his fellow

Taekwondo instructional books (1965)

inmates but of his jailers, too. And within a short time, many were students of the man who had once been expelled from school.

Korea's liberation literally saved Choi, as he was due to be executed three days after the liberation date of August 15, 1945. Within six months he had been commissioned as a second lieutenant in the new South Korean army, and when he was made a company commander in Gwangju, Choi began training his young charges in unarmed self-defense techniques. Choi was now an influential founding presence in the South Korean defense establishment. It was as a military officer that he could return martial arts to the position of relevance they had held to national security as far back as the *hwarang* propagation of the Silla Empire. Upon promotion to first lieutenant in charge of the Second Infantry

TAEKWONDO DAY

The dedication of a particular date on the calendar to commemorate or celebrate an event, occasion, achievement, or cultural facet is especially popular in Korea. There are days to celebrate the national language script (Hangeul), teachers, the first new moon of the year, and even fire prevention, among many others. September 4 is Taekwondo Day. Fittingly, the first Taekwondo Day event held in 2006 was celebrated at Olympic Park in Seoul.

Taekwondo Day was inaugurated as a day on which to rally the world's taekwondoists and the sport's organizers into focusing not just on the their own feats in taekwondo, but as an occasion to consider the sport's destiny. "We have to dream about the future of Taekwondo instead of lingering in the past. In order to do that, we have to join forces all over the world," said Cho Yeong-gi, vice chairman of the KTA at the 2012 Taekwondo Day celebration at the Grand Hilton Hotel in Seoul.

It was on Taekwondo Day, 2009, that the construction of the global home of taekwondo, Muju Taekwondo Park in the northern province of Jeolla, was initiated. Former Kukkiwon President Kang Won-sik described the wider symbolism of the occasion. "I hope that Taekwondo Day will be more than just an event, that it will be a chance for us to understand the importance of harmony and unity."

Taekwondo day ceremony in 2008 © kukkiwon

Regiment at Daejeon, Choi once again commenced systematic instruction in combined martial arts to the soldiers in his regiment. By 1947, he was promoted to captain; soon after he became a major. A Korean martial artist was laying the groundwork for decades of rapid expansion in indigenous martial arts to a generation of soldiers who would go on to fight in one, and in some cases two, major wars. And Choi was also among the very first to demonstrate these methods of self-defense to an interested foreign observer group: US military soldiers stationed in Daejeon. Choi, who became a brigadier general in 1951, would continue to play the major role in the official establishment of taekwondo.

Mudeokgwan in Gyeongsangbuk-do 1966
(source: Korea Taekwondo Association, www.koreataekwondo.org)

An inaugural assembly of ITF (Mar 22 1966)

THE KOREAN WAR

The link between a commonly practiced indigenous martial art form and organized national self-defense in Korea was underlined by the events of the Korean War. The 6.25 War, as called by Koreans because it broke out early on the morning of June 25, 1950, provided the context in which taekwondo experienced a defining growth spurt. In 1952, as fighting continued, South Korean President Syngman Rhee was invited to watch a thirty minute display of martial arts performed by masters in the South Korean army. The performance impressed Rhee so much that afterwards, following discussions with General Choi Hong-hi, he ordered all Korean military personnel to undergo training in martial arts. The result was a boom in the number of schools and institutes offering instruction in the evolving martial arts form.

The most eye-catching feature of the performance had been a bravura display of breaking. Nam Tae-hi had smashed thirteen roof tiles with a single downward punch, startling Korea's president, and giving, to date, the most notable display of the high-flying, high-kicking, tile-breaking demonstration aspects of taekwondo that would come to capture the imagination of a global audience within a few short years. The immediate result of the demonstration was the formation of the Black Tigers, an elite special commando group assembled to fight special ops behind enemy lines. Each member was a trained expert in Choi-inspired martial arts. The long-term result was to reestablish systematic governmental support for martial arts in Korea.

After fighting concluded in 1953, General Choi, who during the conflict had briefed Supreme Commander of United Nations forces General Douglas MacArthur on the frontline situation, organized the 29th Infantry on Jeju Island. This base was to become a center for taekwondo training and produced instructors for the entire army. The 29th Infantry came to be known as the "fist division" because of its map illustration depicting Choi's fist over the Korean Peninsula. It was a crack division skilled to take the fight to the enemy with or without weapons. One technical legacy of the infantry's role is the 29-step move at the red belt testing level of Choi-style taekwondo, a movement named "*Hwarang*." A deeper legacy was a generation of masters produced on the island who taught their skills around the southern half of the peninsula and passed them on to the next generation of Korean soldiers.

THE BIRTH OF TAEKWONDO

More *gwan* were opened following the return to peacetime, the most significant being Odogwan, General Choi's 'The School of My Way.' Inscribed in its self-promoting title, Choi's new *gwan* encapsulated the fundamental contradiction of the rebirth of martial arts in Korea; that during an era of great profusion of schools and rekindled interest in unarmed self-defense, there was no single agreed upon form to practice. The next step was thus to resolve this matter.

Each *gwan* made claim to teach the original Korean martial art, and yet by emphasizing different aspects of *taekkyeon* or *subak*, each gave rise to different terms being applied to their martial art form. There was *soobakdo, kwonbop, taesoodo,* and *tangsoodo,* among others. Each might prove a highly effective martial arts form in its own right, but clearly such inconsistency was not the basis for a single national Korean martial art. In the names of the various styles, however, lay a clue not just to the future name of the unified Korean art but also to its content. *Tangsoodo* means "Way of the Chinese hand" and *taesoodo* "Way of the foot and hand." A compromise would have to be reached that recognized a form combining moves deploying the foot and hand.

The first attempt at unification came at a conference of masters on April 11, 1955. Various persons of importance related to martial arts and sports administration sat down at a meeting arraigned by General Choi to decide upon a name that could be painted on signboards outside schools nationwide. The preferred name was *Taesoodo,* formalizing the idea of the foot and the hand sharing equal importance in the martial art. But the name was not last. Two years later, with one eye fixed firmly on the need for the name of Korea's national martial art to resonate historically, General Choi

preferred the name "Tae-kwon-do" ("The Way of the Hand and Foot") to maintain a dual stress on foot and hand techniques and to establish a linguistic link with the *taekkyeon* of fact, lore, and Korean heritage.

An inaugural assembly of ITF (Mar 22 1966)

KUKKIWON

Kukkiwon : past and present © kukkiwon

The most significant post-war secretariat building of the World Taekwondo Federation was constructed in 1972. At a time when Korean taekwondo's officialdom was zealously pushing the sport overseas, it required a landmark structure to host the sport's administration and foremost events. The million-dollar Kukkiwon World Taekwondo Headquarters was constructed atop a hill in the Gangnam district of Seoul, and stands as a distinctive beacon for taekwondoists everywhere.

The Kukkiwon is a three-story structure capable of accommodating up to 3,000 people to attend various events. Its centerpiece is a *dojang* with seats for spectators on all four sides. The uniqueness of the Kukkiwon building is to be found in the traditional gardens that decorate the structure to its exterior and the use of *giwa*, blue Korean tiles, on its sloping roof, emulating the design of Korea's presidential Blue House. Construction was completed within a year of commencement in November 1971, and celebrated by the attendance of numerous luminaries from the sport and wider Korean society.

The Kukkiwon hosted the first and second World Taekwondo Championships, the first Asian Taekwondo Championships, and many Korean national contests. As the hub of taekwondo's general administration, it has played an important role in the sport's management and propagation. It has hosted international referee and instructor seminars, and the Kukkiwon demonstration team, the latter wowing overseas visitors who seek out the building as a rite of pilgrimage in any taekwondo-related visit to Korea.

ASSOCIATION AND COMPETITION

If the 1950s witnessed taekwondo develop into a single-named branch of the martial arts, the 1960s saw the birth pangs of the new national sport's formal organization. The meeting on April 11, 1955 at which the sport was rudimentarily named had signaled the first major national attempt at association. A board had been formed including leading masters and prominent members of Korean society. But agreement on formal association had not arrived until the start of the next decade. Its development was to have an impact on both taekwondo's rules and goals, as well as its global ethos.

In 1961, the Korean Taesoodo Association governed administrative matters for the various schools. The association gave a new drive to taekwondo's move toward becoming a competitive sport, rather than simply a martial discipline for youth, an unarmed method of self-defense, or a spectacular demonstration activity. The association had been formed by an official decree handed down by the new military government, which ordered the dissenting *gwan* to unify. Taekwondo then made its debut in the Korean National Sports Festival in 1963. This week-long annual inter-city get -together became a national multisport competition in 1934, and although forcibly dissolved by the Japanese colonial government in 1938 and canceled in 1951 due to the Korean War, it remained the premier arena for sports competitors in Korea. The festival was the ideal venue for taekwondo to announce its arrival as a demonstration sport. Taekwondo impressed, and was officially adopted as a permanent sport the following year.

In 1965, the name of the official domestic governing body for the sport was changed to the Korean Taekwondo Association (KTA), and in the same year, the first National Open Korean Taekwondo Championships were held. With the success and rapid proliferation of organized taekwondo, General Choi spied the opportunity to establish taekwondo as the de facto national sport by forming in

1966 the International Taekwondo Federation (ITF). This involved an association of instructors in nine countries: Vietnam, Malaysia, Singapore, West Germany, the United States, Turkey, Italy, Egypt and South Korea. (See Ch. 5) Choi then became the inaugural president of the ITF. The only individual in the country with more influence on taekwondo was the head of its military government.

POLITICS

Taekwondo has been no more averse to the capricious intrusions of politics than any other sport, and this was especially so in its infancy. Lee Won-kuk, founder of Cheongdogwan, exerted a widespread practical and philosophical influence on the direction of taekwondo during the 1940s, and was acknowledged as an organizational force at the highest levels of government. In 1947, the head of South Korea's national police approached Lee as an emissary of President, Syngman Rhee. His offer was simple. If Lee could convince all

ITF Demonstration Team (2007)

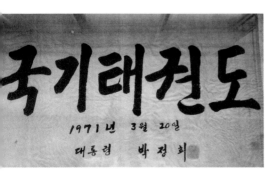

A former president Park Chung-hee composed a calligraphy piece "The national sport: taekwondo" (1971)

5,000 members of his association to join the President's political party, he would be rewarded with the post of minister of internal affairs. Lee's explanation for his refusal epitomizes taekwondo's ethos. "I was concerned that the government's motive for enrolling 5,000 martial artists in the president's party was not to promote justice," he said. Lee, his wife, and several of his top students were subsequently arrested on trumped-up charges of being part of a pro-Japanese group by forces representing a government that had, in its twelve year lifespan, employed scores of ministers identifiable as agents or collaborators under Japanese rule.

Now, over two decades later, General Choi Hong-hi, a soldier who had served at the very highest levels of the country's military during three years of combat with the communist forces of North Korea, was to come into conflict with his country's latest military ruler, Park Chung-hee.

By 1969, the ITF banded the national federations of thirty countries. In his own way, Choi was one of the most well-known Koreans on the international scene. Aside from his military and sports background, he had been made ambassador to the newly independent Malaysia in 1962. But this was also a time in which military provocations by North Korea were occurring against a background of rapid industrialization and economic growth in South Korea. Any philosophical differences Choi harbored with the military regime in Seoul were unlikely to be tolerated. Conspiracies against Choi later went as far as assassination threats. His belief, like that of Lee Won-kuk, that taekwondo is a physical and spiritual way of life unpollutable by temporary national or sectarian forces was not looked on sympathetically by the Park administration. Choi objected to taekwondo being used as an anti-communist propaganda tool. President Park then appointed Kim Un-yong as head of the Korean Taekwondo Association. Kim had played a senior role in the feared Korean Central Intelligence Agency as well as on the Presidential Protection Force. Choi went into exile, considering Canada a sufficiently neutral country from which he could administer the ITF, which now based its headquarters in Toronto. Within a few years ITF membership began to hemorrhage to the newly founded World Taekwondo Federation (WTF). The WTF was established by the Korean government in the belief that the national sport of Korea should have its international umbrella organization based in the homeland rather than abroad. (In 1971, Park Chung-hee wrote "The National Sport Taekwondo" in calligraphy.) The inaugural meeting of the WTF was held in the Kukkiwon, Korea's central taekwondo gym and research center, on May 28, 1973, and its first president was Kim Un-yong. He held the post until 2004.

In the meantime, taekwondo had continued its nationwide rise to competitive prominence. A year after the first National Open Taekwondo Championships, the first National Middle School, High School, University and Individual Taekwondo Championships were held in 1966. Competition among Korea's youth encouraged widespread team and training center formation. In 1970, the first National Elementary School and Women's Taekwondo Championships were held. Within only two decades of being officially named a discrete martial art, taekwondo was ready to take center stage as a competitive sport at the global level and host its own world championships.

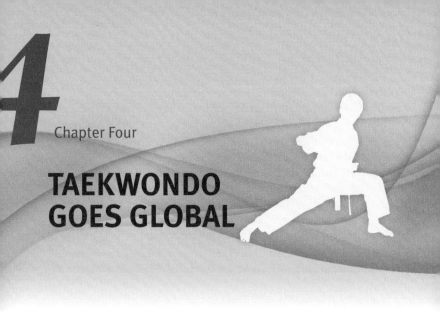

Chapter Four

TAEKWONDO GOES GLOBAL

DEMONSTRATION

In 1945, the Korean Peninsula rid itself of the Japanese yolk. In the process, it unwittingly became one of the world's two split Cold War nations; the newly independent country was a global concern. This meant that formative training in the five *gwan* took place in what was effectively an international arena. The unfortunate divided circumstances of Korea provided an opportunity for the nascent martial art to grab an audience of interested foreign observers. US soldiers based in Daejeon were early witnesses to a method of selling that has served taekwondo effectively ever since: demonstration.

General Choi Hong-hi set about organizing team demonstration tours at home and abroad. He had first given a public demonstration of an evolving unarmed Korean self-defense art while visiting the Fort Riley Ground General School in Kansas in 1949, three years before the more pivotal presentation given to President Syngman Rhee. But as important as America was to become to the international growth of taekwondo, it was the Far East that was first treated to taekwondo visual spectaculars. Over 360,000 spectators turned out to watch Choi's elite black belts, which included Nam Tae-hi, Han Cha-kyo, and Kim Bok-man, give a public demonstration in Vietnam. That trailblazing tour of 1959 also included a stop in Taiwan. Choi was exploiting the confidence of a young art form being spearheaded by masterful pioneers.

Taekwondo goodwill tours purposefully left behind taekwondo teaching centers in every country they visited, seeding the ground for membership of the ITF in years to come. The mid-sixties were a seminal period in taekwondo's self-introduction to a world now seeking contemporary content for its globalized media. Demonstration

Taekwondo demonstraion in Netherlands (1967)

teams visited Singapore, Malaysia, Yugoslavia, Brunei, Hong Kong, and Indonesia in 1964 alone. The following year, they toured Australia, Egypt, Italy, Turkey, and West Germany.

THE TWELVE ORIGINAL MASTERS

One of the KTA's key promotional strategies of the early 1960s was the assembly of twelve elite taekwondo practitioners into a band of demonstration experts. These men, all born in the 1930s and 1940s, were not necessarily the most senior practitioners of martial arts in Korea at the time. But the leaders of the *gwan* from whom the KTA was principally formed included men still practicing the sport under different names, such as *taesoodo*. The twelve original masters, on the other hand, adhered faithfully to the art's recently coined name of taekwondo. A brief survey of their activities reveals the missionary zeal common to taekwondo's early pioneers, as well as the longevity which often accrues to serious students of taekwondo.

TAL (Taekwondo Absolute Legend) World Tour 2011 at the National Theatre in Yangon, Myanmar

The United States

Choi Kwang-jo's entry into martial arts at a young age was spurred by a common enough motivation: a father concerned about his son's frail physical condition. Later on, the small boy who took quickly to unarmed combat was to become chief instructor in the 20th Infantry Division. Choi later moved to the US in pursuit of physical therapies for the injuries he had sustained during decades of taekwondo practice. There he incorporated ideas about physiology and biomechanics into a discrete form of martial arts he called Choi Kwang-Do, "the way of Choi Kwang." He was inducted into the *Tae Kwon Do Times* magazine's Hall of Fame in 2006.

Han Cha-kyo, reputed to be able to jump over a standing opponent, also developed his own system of study, going so far as to obtain patents for the exercises he devised with his brother, Han Min-kyo. Born in 1934, and with strong memories of the Japanese occupation, the Second World War, and the Korean War, Han Cha-kyo spent the 1950s serving the South Korean military as a martial arts instructor. Ultimately achieving 9th *dan*, he combined a military career with the leadership of demonstration teams abroad before emigrating to the US in 1971. There he taught taekwondo in Chicago for many years.

Kong Young-Il trained under taekwondo's formative elite, General Choi and Nam Tae-hi. Subsequently Kong was an important member of Choi's globetrotting demonstration teams, eventually visiting over a hundred countries. Originally a karate and judo expert, Kong' altered his martial arts emphasis while serving in the military between 1963 and 1967. The end of the sixties saw Kong and his brother settle in the US, where they founded Young Brothers Taekwondo Associates, and Kong later was a master instructor for the FBI. He was, during a lifetime dedicated to taekwondo, given the All-American Open Award, inducted into the taekwondo Hall of Fame, voted Martial Artist of the Year, and promoted to 9th *dan* in 1997 by General Choi.

Canada

Choi Chang-keun, like so many students in taekwondo's formative years, learned his skills in the military, attaining the rank of 2nd *dan* by 1960. At the heart of taekwondo's technical and stylistic developments, he helped Choi Hong-hi devise many of the Chang Hon patterns the following year. After teaching in Malaysia and participating in demonstrations around the world, Choi Chang-keun moved to Canada in 1970, opening the first taekwondo school in Vancouver. He achieved 9th *dan* in 2002, and late in life was still campaigning to reunite ITF practitioners across the world.

Another member of the exodus to Canada was the late Park Jung-tae. Schooled Western boxing before learning taekwondo as a child, Park was elevated to the senior administrative role of president of the Korean Taesoodo Association, as it was then called, in his early twenties. He instructed soldiers in Vietnam before moving to Toronto in 1970, establishing the Manitoba Taekwondo Association. Having played an advanced role in the organization of the sport since his youth, Park was liable to play a part in taekwondo's political fissures, and founded the Global Taekwondo Federation (GTF) following disagreement with the ITF over inter-Korean issues in 1990. Park died in 2002 and received an honorary 9th *dan*.

INNOVATORS

A number of taekwondo's original masters branched out after resettling abroad. Kim Kwang-Il developed a hinterland of interests aside from his professional dedication to taekwondo. Kim was originally instrumental in the popularization of taekwondo in West Germany, which already had a competitive martial arts market at the time. Kim typifies the big personalities of the taekwondo pioneers in

Lee Jong-hyup, Kim Jong-chan, Kim Young-ho, Choi Hong-hi, Nam Tae-hi (1964)

Taekwondo demonstraion in Germany (1967)

the way he took to life in a very different culture. He ran a restaurant in his adopted city of Stuttgart for a number of years, having completed training as a brewmeister, and therein doubling his total of masters' status.

Kim Jong-chan was another taekwondo pioneers who demonstrated as far afield as Malaysia and Argentina. He was a 7th *dan* teacher and another émigré, his preferred second country being Canada. Kim Jong-chan became administratively involved with a distant offshoot of taekwondo called *tukido*, which describes itself as a martial art whose "movements are based on the fact that all force derives from the feet pushing off the floor."

Europe

Like Kim Jong-chan, Park Jong-soo became a pivotal figure in the rise of taekwondo's popularity in Western Europe. In 1965, Park responded positively to the German Taekwondo Association's invitation to be its coach before going on to found the Netherlands

Taekwondo Association a year later. A perennial member of General Choi's demonstration team, Kim had been another pioneer to emerge from the South Korean military a taekwondo master, becoming Korea national champion in 1964. By the turn of the seventies, Park was established in Toronto, home of General Choi's ITF. Disagreement over relations with North Korea resulted in a twenty-year rift in their relationship, however; the rift was healed before Choi passed away. Despite disagreements over the question of taekwondo in North Korea, the man who held seminars in Beijing and Afghanistan can never have been said to be restrictive in his beliefs about spreading taekwondo abroad.

Most of the original masters retained a relationship with the ITF, but Park Sun-jae eventually stepped outside of its orbit. He was elected acting president of the WTF following the resignation of Kim Un-yong, having worked since 1968 for the promotion of taekwondo in Italy. Park Sun-jae was already much traveled before then and had presented seminars in Croatia, but it was in Italy where he chose to concentrate his taekwondo roots. Eventually he

Korean Taekwondo demonstration team in Italy (1965)

became president of the Federazione Italiana Taekwondo.

Rhee Ki-ha was central to the development of British and Irish taekwondo. He first came into contact with British students while training Royal Air Force personnel stationed in Singapore in the mid 1960s. They invited him to teach in the UK and in 1967, Rhee founded the UKTA. He adopted the honorific title of "First" Grand Master Rhee when General Choi, who described Rhee as "the best ever student of taekwondo," conferred 9th *dan* status on him in 1997.

The Rhee Brothers

Australians know the "father of taekwondo" not to be General Choi but rather Rhee Chong-chul, who arrived in Adelaide following his concerted efforts to promote taekwondo in Southeast Asia. The former Marine instructor garnered a reputation for personally conducting the Rhee Taekwondo School grading examinations across Australia and New Zealand. This dedication, together with representation on numerous committees (Park was chairman of the Oceana Division of the Advisory Council on Democratic and Peaceful Unification, chairman of the Seoul Olympics Supporting Committee, and founding president of the Korean Community Hall Construction Supporting Committee) resulted in governmental recognition with the 2003 Dongbaeg Medal for the promotion of Korean culture.

Rhee's brother and fellow original master Chong-hyup assisted in the founding of the Rhee Taekwondo School system. He arrived in Australia a little later than his older brother, but had worked to promote taekwondo in the same regions of the world. Together they built up the largest set of taekwondo schools in Australia. At least twenty-five Rhee students went on to found their own martial arts schools.

Korean Festival in Sydney, Australia (2010)

LEGACY

The original twelve masters were fundamental in the storied rise of taekwondo to the role of world's most popular martial art. Not only were they the primary agents for the art's dissemination, they were also responsible for a wider introduction to the world of the Korean people, language, and culture. However, there were other personal and political reasons, push as well as pull factors, for the almost 100 percent emigration rate of these men. "In Korea, there [were] restrictions [on] going to other countries," said Kong Young-Il in an interview. "If you lived in the USA, you could travel anywhere. That is what convinced me to move. I had a vision to introduce taekwondo to the world and did not like the restrictions that Koreans had on traveling to other countries." The timing of their decisions to make lives in foreign countries did not automatically follow on the heels of a developing career pattern of military teaching and membership in Choi Hong-hi's demonstration team; they were the culmination of a period of philosophical and ideological tensions with the military government in South Korea, which were best dealt with non-confrontationally in foreign climes.

Though scattered to the four corners of the earth, the twelve original masters were bonded by points in common that have guided the principles of taekwondo to this day. Their participation in spectacular demonstrations has established taekwondo as the martial art that continues to monopolize the wow factor. Their advancement to 9th *dan* is a practical inspiration for taekwondo students around the world. Their family-centeredness and business entrepreneurialism has helped root taekwondo in the real world, so that taekwondo has avoided becoming an esoteric practice or cloistered vocation. In establishing broad reaching schools, many of the twelve original masters have left a tangible legacy for taekwondo's future. They have also encouraged, through their theoretical and practical adaptations, the idea that taekwondo is mutable, that it is an art open to creative interpretation, despite their loyal tendency to Choi Hong-hi's ITF style of combat. The twelve original masters, many of whom were still alive, well, and teaching at the time of writing, embodied taekwondo from its formal inception to the Seoul Olympics.

Poomse training in Chile © kukkiwon

FATHER OF TAEKWONDO IN US

Taekwondo has been Korea's most successful soft power export, a spectacular harbinger of national "brand value." It is the near ancestor of the "hallyu" phenomenon, the so-called Korean Wave of popular cultural exports across Asia and as far as France and Latin America, which includes mostly movies and K-pop. Taekwondo got there first. But to achieve its global status, it had to penetrate the strongest soft power nation on earth. Embodying the brazen confidence necessary to the task was one of taekwondo's most colorful characters, Jhoon Rhee. Acknowledged as the father of taekwondo in the United States, Jhoon made the presence of taekwondo felt at the highest levels of American life for decades.

His taekwondo story begins with a stock tale of youthful humiliation. When the six-year old Rhee returns to his mother complaining that a five-year old girl has physically bested him, his mother scolds the boy. The frail kid begins pushups, lifting weights, and the study of traditional martial arts. Despite enjoying the privilege of studying under Won Kuk-lee of Cheongdogwan, Rhee had to deal with taekwondo being associated with street hoodlums, an image that he, after completing military service, wished to eradicate on a hemispherical scale. So he arrived in Texas in 1956 with $46 in his pocket, in a town where most locals had never even seen an Asian, and began his struggles with the language, it being a side ambition of Rhee's to become an accomplished public speaker, the better to proselytize his faith in taekwondo.

A breakthrough moment for Rhee and the fate of taekwondo in

Jhoon Rhee and Muhammad Ali (1976)

Jhoon Rhee and his students in Washington D.C. (1995)

America arrived in 1965 with the misfortune of one congressman from Cleveland, who is mugged on the streets of Washington, D.C. Rhee hears the story and contacts the politician's office, offering to provide one-on-one taekwondo lessons so that the Congressman will not so easily fall victim again. The lessons Rhee provides are free, with one proviso. The congressman is to spread news about the benefits of this new martial art to his constituency and beyond, to use his position, in other words, as a soapbox for the promotion of the sport.

In the following 45 years, Rhee went on to instruct 350 members of Congress in taekwondo, rising at 5 a.m. three mornings a week to meet his commitments. The grandmaster took naturally to his celebrity status, and in time was approached to inculcate in other world-class combatants the benefits of a taekwondo-infused multidisciplinary approach. He trained world heavyweight champion Muhammad Ali, assisting the boxer in refining his block techniques. He got acquainted with Bruce Lee, the peerless martial arts movie star, to whom Rhee offers tips on kicking. Lee, in turn, introduced Rhee to producers seeking to make a movie centered around this relatively new Korean martial art, a project which eventually became the film *When Taekwondo Strikes* starring Rhee and released in 1973.

Rhee conducted his popular media and celebrity status to complement a systematic teaching of taekwondo in over 60 schools. As he aged, his renown only increased, and he was the subject of an introductory speech given in his honor by President George H. Bush. By this time, Rhee was pushing taekwondo to the fore as a bridge between superpowers, traveling to the USSR, meeting with President Gorbachev, and establishing a number of schools far behind the Iron Curtain. This earned him a World Peace Award from his Moscow hosts.

Back in the United States, 30,000 fans attended a concert given in his tribute. It came as little surprise when a 'Jhoon Rhee Day' was established. On his 80th birthday, Rhee entertained television crews by smashing a tile with a powerful "accu-punch" then doing 100 pushups in under a minute. Memories of the humiliation he received at the hands of a five-year old girl have been vanquished on a world stage. At 81, he was still practicing for an hour each day. He introduced Americans to his wider philosophy and hopes for the world in a tome called *Trutopia*. This once penurious man, who had arrived in Texas with the goal of perhaps opening one or two schools, is now expounding his belief in human perfectability, based on a common sense approach to life in which mankind never knowingly makes mistakes. He tells all who will listen of his plans to live to the age of 136.

THE FIRST WORLD CHAMPIONSHIPS

The 1970s were a period in which the WTF established its administrative hold on taekwondo internationally, and the

Kukkiwon directed sport and competition-oriented taekwondo laid the foundations for demonstration status at the 1988 Olympics. The landmark competition of the decade was the first World Championships, organized by the Korean Taekwondo Association, and staged at the Seoul Kukkiwon. The event attracted over 200 competitors from 19 countries on five continents. Korea took first place in the medals table, but the competition was made memorable by the skills of Joe Hayes, captain of the US team that placed second. Hayes dominated North American taekwondo at this time, and was famed for his fierce reverse punch and spectacular mid-flight spinning capabilities, which were compared in film with the movements of ballet dancer Rudolf Nuryev. Hayes had already been inducted into the prestigious Black Belt Hall of Fame in 1972, and received plaudits from admirer Bruce Lee. As a figure in taekwondo's history, Hayes embodied the individual talents taekwondo could produce, as well as the remarkable lobbying and promotion skills of a country that could globalize its new national sport within two decades of a shattering civil war.

2nd World Taekwondo Championships (1975)

TAEKWONDO PEACE CORPS

In 2012, the World Taekwondo Federation (WTF) was nominated for the International Sports Federation of the Year Award in the Peace and Sport International Forum in Sochi, Russia, home of the 2014 Winter Olympics. Key to its nomination was the international community work and development undertaken by the federation's Taekwondo Peace Corps.

The WTF established the corps in 2008 with the goal of promoting peace through cultural understanding and the spreading of Olympic values across the globe. By the time of its nomination, nearly a thousand young volunteers had been dispatched to 174 locations in 86 countries.

At the core of the Peace Corps ethos is the application of taekwondo's disciplining ethic to disadvantaged youth in developing countries to foster self-belief, a broader outlook, and the will to succeed. Initially, the WTF dispatched 27 Korean university students majoring in taekwondo to Russia, Paraguay, India, Pakistan, and China in 2008. They then spent the summer teaching locals the skills and values of taekwondo. The program proved to be such a success that in winter of the same year, thirty-two more Peace Corps members were sent to eight more countries.

The Peace Corps aim their activites in regions of countries with little or no permanent sports infrastructure in place, so exposing communities not just to the benefits of studying taekwondo but the wider advantages of organised sport. To ensure that the goals of the Peace Corps are a permanent achievement, the WTF is planning to create regional and local Taekwondo Peace Corps. This will root the sport within the community, foster the

multigenerational reach of the programs, and allow individual communities to better finely tune the local character of the organization.

In tutoring young people as far as Bolivia, East Timor, and Uzbekistan, the Taekwondo Peace Corps earned the attention of United Nations Secretary General Ban Ki-moon. "Through its mission as a sport and development activities such as the World Taekwondo Peace Corps, the WTF has done a great job in promoting education of youth, gender equality, healthy living, cross-cultural understanding and international cooperation, so that anyone who wishes to participate can reach for their dreams in life."

World Taekwondo Peace Corps members in Fiji (left) and El Salvador (right)
© World Taekwondo Peace Corps

THE ROAD TO OLYMPICS

Korea's taekwondo authorities meticulously set about pursuing the global sports administrative procedure necessary for IOC recognition. In the United States, prominent Korean instructors had taekwondo admitted to the Amateur Athletic Union (AAU), which then adopted the WTF's technical standards. Meanwhile the first Asian Taekwondo Championships were held in Seoul in October 1974. The following year, taekwondo became an affiliate member of the General Association of International Sports Federation (GAISF), an association with direct ties to the IOC. Then in 1976, further recognition came as the International Military Sports Council (CISM) adopted taekwondo as its 23rd official sport in the World Military Championships.

   Regional championships, demonstrating taekwondo's reach, popularity, and organizing autonomy, were crucial to any bid for Olympic status, and in May 1976, the first European Taekwondo Championships were held in Barcelona, Spain. The first Pan-American Taekwondo Championships were held in Mexico City, Mexico, in 1978, and the first African Taekwondo Championships

1st Asian Taekwondo Championships (1974)

were held in Abidjan, Ivory Coast, in 1979. When WTF President Kim Un-Young was elected chairman of the World Federation of Non-Olympic Sports in 1979, it was an acknowledgement of Kim and the WTF as leading-edge sports body administrators

2011 Pan-American Games in Guadalajara, Mexico

and a stepping stone on the promotion of taekwondo to its patriotic goal: full Olympic status.

On July 17, 1980, in its 83rd session held in Moscow during that city's hosting of the Games of the XXII Olympiad, which, ironically, South Korea was boycotting in solidarity with twenty other nations protesting the Soviet Union's invasion of Afghanistan, the International Olympic Committee formally recognized the WTF. Taekwondo then featured in the 1981 World Games as an official sport, and having featured in other global sports competitions such as the 1986 Asian Games in Seoul and the 1987 Pan-American Games in Indianapolis, 120 male and 63 female athletes from 34 countries competed in taekwondo at the demonstration level in the Seoul Olympics in 1988, held, fittingly enough, in South Korea's capital.

The hosts used the event as the opportunity for a gigantic choreographed demonstration, producing in the opening ceremony for the watching billions, in what were the first Olympics not to suffer from a major boycott for decades, a captivating display of taekwondo bravura. The competition ran in eight weight classes, and was attended by 243 taekwondo instructors and 58 officials from WTF member associations.

Taekwondo was now touching the world of sport everywhere, and went on to feature in the Goodwill Games, the Southeast Asian Games, the Central American and Caribbean Games, and the South Pacific Games. Taekwondo had long since shed the soubriquet of "Korean karate," which had been employed as an advertising expedient by its propagators to attract youth from who had numerous competing martial arts to choose from. Taekwondo appeared on the after-school curriculum of high schools across the world, popular with parents for imbuing young men, in particular, with a respect for seniority, a structured outlet for adolescent aggression, and a regular and relatively cheap form of physical exercise. The Korean flag *taeguki* hung next to Old Glory in the United States and taekwondo became second only to soccer in certain Middle Eastern and Central American nations. Its reputation for reputedly boosting students concentration, extending good health in older practitioners, and, depending on the *dojang*, offering a path to the holistic rewards of meditation, resulted, after an explosion in competition and association, in taekwondo being adopted as an official sport of the Sydney 2000 Olympic Games at the 103rd IOC Session in Paris in 1994.

South Korean Taekwondo practitioner Hwang Kyung-Seon. She is a two-time Olympic Champion from 2008 and 2012 Summer Olympics.

KOREAN TIGERS

A young man and woman embrace. The sound of traditional pipe melodies signals that they are in love. Suddenly the music takes on an ominous tenor and the scene changes. Four young men in black *dobok* appear from under dry ice to threaten the couple. What follows is an expertly choreographed display of fighting techniques in which the couple successfully defend their honor from an unruly mob. As an art form, it is practically a standalone genre, combining narrative, music, dance, aerobics and, at its center, the martial art of taekwondo. This is the Korean Tigers demonstration team, a world-renowned troupe of martial artists that has been exhibiting traditional Korean physical culture globally since its inception in 1990.

The Tigers were originally formed with the idea of being the most representative of Korea's taekwondo demonstration teams. They have performed in many countries and at most of the world's key sporting taekwondo events, including the world championships and the Sydney Olympics.

© KTigers

The first demonstration teams were renowned for their expert team coordination, but choreography was characteristically rigid and simple. The Tigers have evolved the form, incorporating every genre suited to a modern theatrical stage performance. Their goal is to present to the audience not just an exhibition of spectacular martial arts but a futuristic union of timeless physical feats and the mass appeal of contemporary entertainment.

The tiger is the third of 12 animals in Eastern astrology. As well as symbolizing a protector it is also an omen of good luck, and tiger imagery is therefore common in everyday Korean life (the animal was an emblem of the Seoul Olympics in 1988). Though tigers were a source of folk fear when they roamed the peninsula, sculptures of tigers are sometimes still placed around tombs. During the Korean War (1950–53) one of the most famous commando groups of martial arts trained soldiers formed to fight the communist forces of North Korea was called the Black Tigers. The Korean Tigers, with their fearsome workmanship and technological artistry, renews again this tradition of the tiger's cultural significance.

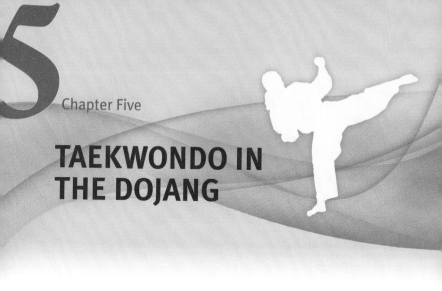

5

TAEKWONDO IN THE DOJANG

ITF AND WTF TAEKWONDO

In 1965, Choi Hong-hi published his English-language guide to the young martial art, *Taekwon-do: The Art of Self-Defense*, in which he included the original *Chang-hon* patterns, "Chang-hon" being the his own penname. Taekwondo form patterns (*hyeong*) are called *teul* in ITF taekwondo and are considered as a guide to a basic history of Korea. Those original 24 *teul* form the basis of ITF taekwondo, which is sometimes called "traditional taekwondo." The Cheon-ji pattern (literally "heaven and earth") is the first pattern and includes 19 movements. The beginner is figuratively describing the beginning of creation, through a series of blocks and punches.

A signature feature of ITF taekwondo in the *dojang* was the practice of executing a technique and performing it at full speed, but stopping just short of the target contact point. Choi believed that such momentum control would result in a more effective martial artist than one who executed through the target. This non-contact form of approach to combat would hamper any martial art seeking global institutional recognition as a competitive sport, resembling as it might to the untutored eye a kind of "shadow fighting." Also, the ITF was created by Choi as an independent organization, under his presidency, to teach the *Chang-hon* style described in his book. The one-man origins of the organization's founding consequently left the ITF vulnerable to rifts and splits and two ITF organizations began competing for legitimacy, though both adhered to the original *Chang-hon teul.*

The WTF, on the other hand, is a sport governing body. It establishes competition rules and regulates tournaments. As such, the WTF and not the ITF is recognized by the International Olympic Committee, and it is the WTF that coordinates the

The 5th World Youth Taekwondo Camp (Jul 2013)

national member associations of member countries. In WTF taekwondo, patterns are called *poomsae* and the first eight of the seventeen are called *taegeuk* patterns (certain schools use a different first eight called *poomsae palgwe*). The unity of yin and yang is called *taegeuk* in Korean, and each *taegeuk* is diagramatically represented by a different trigram, a set of three lines, open and closed, taken from the hexagrams of the I Ching (and which feature on the South Korean national flag, the *taegeukki*). WTF taekwondo is often referred to, though not always disparagingly, as "sport taekwondo." The Kukkiwon in Seoul, the single-purpose taekwondo gymnasium in South Korea, served as the headquarters of the WTF until the opening of Muju Taekwondo Park in the North Jeolla Province in 2013. The Kukkiwon frames the official curriculum of taekwondo taught in instructor certification courses, and the style of taekwondo seen at the Olympics is what might be called Kukki-taekwondo.

It is easy and erroneous, however, to overstress the differences between ITF and WTF taekwondo. The patterns have different names and there are variations in Romanized spelling for certain terms; but it is not as if the members of an ITF-style school in Chicago might fail to recognize the martial art being practiced by members of a Kukki-style school in Seoul. The exigencies of competition have brought about different emphases in approach but the origin is one.

TECHNICAL DEVELOPMENT

Early pioneer Nam Tae-hi, who so impressed President Syngman Rhee with a thirteen-tile break in the famous 1952 demonstration, said of taekwondo's formative years, "In the early days, taekwondo consisted of ten hand and eight kicking techniques, all aimed at the vital points of the body...The hand techniques were punch, spear hand, palm, knife hand, inner ridge hand, twin fingers, single finger, back fist and tiger fist. The kicking techniques consisted of front, side, round and back kick and these were aimed at various levels of the body." The complicated spins and shuffles of the Olympic era were an age away.

But there was, as was common to martial arts across China and Japan and in a brutal reminder of taekwondo's wartime deployment, a strike known as spear hand or straight fingertip, a blow which, when applied with the addition of a half-twist corkscrew to penetrate an enemy's skin, could kill. The foot could also be used lethally, and by applying its heel or outside edge in the lead-leg side kick, a "foot sword" could immobilize opponents, breaking bones in the process. The aim in real combat was to strike once, not two or three times, and without the requirement of space to build momentum.

As taekwondo developed, it began to self-consciously contradistinguish itself from its *tangsoodo* (literally 'Way of the Chinese Hand', ie. karate) and *taekkyeon* roots. Indeed, despite Choi Hong-hi naming the art to resonate linguistically with one of Korea's major ancient martial arts, there was little obvious relationship. *Taekkyeon* had no elbow or hand strikes and did not concentrate on attacks to vital areas. Although it utilized hand blocks, there were no full powered kicks. *Taekkyeon* centered around pushes, stamps, jumps, and leg sweeps.

Yet as Choi's art transmuted into taekwondo, there was still a tendency to embroider the martial artists of cave paintings and ancient documents with superhuman capacities. The general himself talked of his ancestors kicking a ceiling after jumping from a sitting position. However, in Choi's extension of shotokan karate founder Gichin Funashoki's idea that power comes from rotating the hips to put weight into a punch, taekwondo's founder was acknowledging a more directly related forebear.

Choi's adaptation was that the martial artist must pull the non-punching hand backwards with a force equal to that of the punching hand to maximize striking force. His innovation was formulated to increase power. Indeed, Choi described his theory of power as being scientifically based, and cited Newton's third law of motion, which states that every action has an equal and opposite reaction when insisting on the need for the non-punching hand to match the punching hand in force. Choi's theory had six parts: reaction force, the Newtonian idea of equal power; concentration; equilibrium, in other words maintaining one's center of gravity; breath control; mass; and most importantly because it unites the other five, speed. In other words, a smaller man, such as the 100 pounds Choi was, might generate more power and hence defeat a slower heavyweight. And nothing encapsulated the demonstration of this precept for all to see better than an expert show of tile breaking.

Choi, in his first descriptions of taekwondo, was ever keen to find metaphors in learning, especially in science and military strategy. The "cycle of taekwondo" described the art's main disciplines as analogous with army processes.

> 1. Fundamental exercises are to taekwondo what an individual soldier's basic training is to his military skills.
> 2. *Dallyon*, the hardening of attacking tools, is like a soldier's basic maintenance of equipment.
> 3. *Teul/Poomsae* patterns correlate with platoon tactics.
> 4. Sparring amounts to a field exercise in simulated combat conditions.
> 5. Self-defense is real combat.

The "Sine Wave," taken from the mathematical curve that describes a smooth repetitive oscillation, is the fundamental movement at the heart of taekwondo maneuvers and patterns. It is related to the theory of power, and is a technique of motion that teaches the student to use mass as well as acceleration to gain maximum power. The basic sine wave is a down, up, down motion. The muscles are relaxed and tensed as the student keeps arms and legs bent while maneuvering center of mass through the motion. Meanwhile knee spring allows that center to travel along a curve before dropping the weight into the strike.

Publication of the *teul*, the theory of power, the cycle of taekwondo, and the sine wave was the beginning of a process which

ITF demonstration Team

would end with academic degrees being offered in taekwondo. On the practical front, Woo Jong-lim's reverse turning kick was eagerly adopted by Choi, and as the early masters experimented with airborne and 180-degree kicks, a number made their way into Choi's book.

Present-day taekwondo would look quite different to a practitioner of the 40s and 50s. As taekwondo developed, a shift in emphasis from pattern and form practice to sport-combat sparring was accelerated by a demotion of the status of the block. Taekwondo evolved in the heat of competitive experimentation and competitors learned, through advanced techniques in footwork, to kick at the same time as their attacker. By doing so, they could counter an attack almost simultaneous with the attack itself, and the block was largely set aside as an unnecessary expedient of defense. Herein lies the crux of the debate regarding taekwondo as sport versus taekwondo as martial art. Those who argue for a retention of taekwondo's essence claim that sport taekwondo produces young martial artists able to churn out a flurry of impressive successive spinning kicks at the expense of hand work. They point out how competitors' arms will hang limply by their side; and that banning hand-to-head techniques prevents development of a good guard and offensive handwork strategy. In other words, the art of self-defense is lost. They argue that instead, students must start developing power, Choi's theoretical core, from their first day in the *dojang*...

IN THE DOJANG

It would be exaggerating to suggest that a taekwondo gym is a holy place, but there are sacral elements to the ritual of discipline most teachers demand of their students as soon as they step across the *dojang* entrance mat. Some or all of the following might constitute a standard code of *dojang* behavior.

Members acknowledge the flags upon entering by bowing in their direction (many *dojang* will have their national flag and the South Korean flag prominently displayed side by side on a main wall). Students line up according to rank and seniority, with the most senior ranking member flanking the instructor and calling out commands as they both face the class. Flags are saluted and the instructor bowed to before a short meditation. In South Korea, and elsewhere, students might recite a short pledge to the country and the sport before commencing a regular training session.

The greeting, and the style of its execution, is repeated at dismissal. Salutation is of signal importance in relations between students and instructors and between students and one another. Breaking the frame of the class by losing self-control or patience is greatly frowned upon and considered unacceptable, along with persistent unnecessary noise. During exercise or contests, students are expected to turn back to face their opponent or instructor, correctly adjust their *dobok* (uniform), and issue the appropriate salutation; where possible, Korean terminology is to be used.

The need for propriety extends to general physical posture. While sitting on the floor in a crossed leg position, students should place hands on knees and keep a straight back when not directly engaged in training. Students are expected to keep their *dobok* clean and pressed and have finger and toe nails clipped short to prevent injury. More general precepts and prohibitions might include the need to gain permission to leave the *dojang* at any point during class; no jewelry, profanity, chewing gum, smoking or drinking in class; bowing to the master instructor when entering the master instructor's office; never calling the master instructor by first name; and the formal addressing of instructors and black belt ranking members.

Warm up and warm down routines vary from *dojang* to *dojang*, but might involve joint rotation exercises (head, arms, hips, knees), basic stretches such as the butterfly stretch and partial or full splits, exercises designed to improve flexibility, squats and dead lifts, as well as basic forms such as abdominal crunches and pushups. Although the level of Korean used in non-Korean *dojang* may vary from none to total, one commonly learned aspect is the Korean counting system, which is used in warm up and drilling.

Now the student is ready to be ready.

A *dojang* in Senegal

POOMSAE

The Ready Position (준비 joonbi)

The initial position is designed to concentrate the mind and fill the body with energy. The stance begins by moving the left foot so that the feet are one shoulder length apart, and, with a deep breath, raising the hands to chest level. Fists should then be closed and lowered to be level with the lower abdomen. The space between the fists as well as between the fists and the lower abdomen should now be approximately one fist long. The chin is lowered slightly, and sight is directed ahead. The student maintains a straight posture.

Stance is called *seogi*, and the taekwondo practitioner assumes one or reverts to one during patterns and sparring. A commonly reverted to initial stance during sparring is the fighting stance, which will leave the student erect enough to maneuver into a kick without the need to adjust the legs, so telegraphing the next move to the opponent. The front stance and back stance are also commonly used in sparring, while the horse riding stance, for example, is more appropriate for forms and patterns.

Kicking (차기 chagi)

Olympic practitioners and black-belt taekwondoists are capable of the most elaborate and explosive, gymnastic-kicking maneuvers, such as the 540 kick, which involves one and a half mid-air spins before executing, say, a back spinning hook kick. Or their sheer speed allows such rapid shuffling of the feet that they can present themselves closer to the opponent before executing a full force axe kick. But long before the student is capable of run-jumping into the air and launching a side piercing kick, he or she must practice thousands of times the sub motions and full maneuvers of the core basic taekwondo kicks. The back kick is believed to be the most powerful kick available to the taekwondoist, and so its successful execution is of great and intimidating use, though if the motion is too big, the opponent has a prime opportunity for a counterattacking maneuver. Half moon and spinning kicks, also known as crescent and hook kicks, in which the foot is lifted from the ready position to an angle of 45 degrees and then dragged inside like a parabola before an axe kick is executed, require intense concentrated dexterity. Meanwhile the push kick, in which the target is kicked straight on with a foot bottom facing front, is a popular tournament kick. Taekwondo has a number of basic kicks.

(left) *joonbi* (right) *chagi*

The Front Kick (앞차기 apchagi)

The fundamental principle of all kicks is clear in executing the front kick. The knee should be raised to an angle of 90 degrees, though its final position depends on the height of the target. The front under sole of the foot is used to connect with vertical targets, such as the solar plexus and jaw, whilst the top of the foot aims for horizontal targets such as the genitals or a practice target. The front kick should be executed with a straight waist, to provide more power. Force is put into the ankle and toes to keep the leg straight, and to not diffuse power. The angle of the supporting foot when the waist is turned as the kick is delivered is crucial. The ideal angle is 45 degrees. It is important to hold the waist back when delivering an effective front kick, and a supporting foot angle of less than 45 degrees means the waist has not been pulled back enough. In a practice scenario, the taekwondoist then resumes the ready position.

Effective front foot exercises include practicing the kick while hopping on the supporting foot; kick and retrieve balance practice, in which the target is struck with fast, short kicks; and consecutive kicks with both feet, where the upper body is straight, and low kicks are practiced first.

The Side Kick (옆차기 yeopchagi)

This is an important kick in the taekwondo player's armory. Starting from the ready position, the body should be turned slightly. The knee is raised and then kept close to the body to make the attack tight and strong. At this point, the supporting foot is turned to an angle of 170 to 180 degrees. The kicking leg is then stretched forcefully and the kick is executed with the outer part of the foot. It is important that the foot go straight to the target and not in a curved motion, to maximize the outlay of force. Finally, the kicking foot is drawn back and the ready position assumed. As usual, the relationship between the upper body and the foot is crucial in maintaining balance, and thus, the kick should be practiced many times, with a focused dedication to mastering each of the sub motions. The side kick is a core taekwondo movement, and a student's basic ability can be judged by observing execution of this maneuver.

Effective exercises include holding a chair while performing the kick to practice maintaining balance; repeating the side kick at low levels before graduating to higher targets; and lying down to practice strengthening leg stretching power and angle correction.

The Roundhouse (돌려차기 dollyeochagi)

This kick is used most frequently in competitive matches. The initial sub motion is identical with that of the front kick, as the knee is lifted up to an angle of 90 degrees. By twisting the waist and front part of the foot, the leg is turned to an angle of 180 degrees, as the supporting foot quickly maneuvers its angle. The kicking leg should now be parallel to the ground while the waist should be in a straight line with the supporting foot. Key to the roundhouse is achieving a parallel relationship between the kicking leg and the floor; keeping the waist and thigh in a toward position; and the snapping movement of the blow. The effectiveness of a roundhouse kick is enhanced by the application of spiral force, twisting the striking part of the body as it connects with the target to concentrate and internalize the effect of the blow. Mere straight line contact will disperse the force, whilst a spiraling blow will greatly increase effectiveness.

Effective roundhouse exercises include lying on the side and kicking repeatedly using only the lower leg; kicking a target held by a partner, who should hold a second target in his or her other hand that the student must avoid to practice straight rather than curved kicks; and to reduce the kicking angle and shorten the distance to the target, fast kicks in which the leg is lifted straight up to kick at waist height.

(clockwise from top) *apchagi* © kukkiwon, *dollyeochagi, yeopchagi*

PUNCHES AND STRIKES

Taekwondo is not, of course, solely a kicking martial art. In very close combat, it may not be inappropriate to attempt a kick, and a punching strike will prove more effective. A basic jab involves a flick of the fist on the forward arm (the thumb being rested over the middle and third finger of the closed fist). Upper cuts and hooks are similar to those punches found within the traditional boxer's armory, whilst the back fist strike uses the back of the hand to attack the opponent. The momentum of the body turning around will deliver additional power, and so this strike may be delivered as a spinning back fist.

The bare hand, unencumbered by gloves, is a more adaptable weapon. The fingers can be pinched into position or extended, as in the knife hand strike, in which the outer side of the hand, fingers clasped together, is chopped down onto the opponent's neck or other soft areas. The inner side is used in the ridge hand strike, sometimes called a reverse knife hand strike. In other strikes, such as the palm strike, the fingers are scarcely utilized, while elbow strikes do not use the hand at all.

Blocks (막기 makgi)

Though less a feature of taekwondo in sporting competition, blocking is a cornerstone of self-defense techniques, and the taekwondoist has a wide variety of blocks to deploy. An open hand block, such as the knife hand block, enables a student to both block and then grab an opponent's leg or wrist. Again using an open hand, the downward palm block uses the palm to block an incoming kick. The closed-fist low block and high block are used by bringing the outside of the forearm down or up, respectively, to protect against attacks. "Double" blocks often involve the student crossing arms into an "X" to protect from kicks to the groin or higher attacks. Kicks themselves can be used as blocks, and the push kick is an effective method of blocking an opponent's forward momentum. Therefore a block can be an attacking maneuver if achieved with sufficient accuracy and power.

Breaks (격파 gyeokpa)

Breaking may be a feature of belt grading tests. Wooden boards may be broken with kicks or punches and a few techniques should to be born in mind by the practicing student. The student should aim for a point past the board, so that they punch or kick through it. In other words, momentum should be maintained beyond the physical barrier of the object. Accuracy should be practiced, especially to avoid an accident in which the board holder is struck. Re-breakable plastic boards are a safe option for practicing at home. Taekwondo shoes are available to prevent injury during board breaking practice. It is a good idea to infuse this aspect of taekwondo with a creative element, and older students in particular should vary their breaking routine.

(left) *makgi* © kukkiwon (right) *gyeokpa*

TRAINING

The key to any martial art, as with all human endeavors, is to master the basics and then practice. Repetition and physical conditioning form the groundwork for any taekwondoist who aspires to rise through the belts in peak shape. Light free weights with maximum repetitions are recommended in the gym; stationary machines for leg muscle building. For general stamina, an obvious essential practice is not to skip classes. Otherwise, traditional exercises such as running (short sprints rather than distances); bicycling, including hill climbs, jumping jacks, squat thrusts, and lateral jumps are all relevant to the taekwondo student's specific conditioning needs. Plyometric exercises, in particular, add power and the ability to quickly maneuver from a static position. So medicine ball throws, vertical jumps, clap pushups and lateral box jumps, in which the student jumps from side to side over an object, are all supporting aids to the serious taekwondoist.

Specific tips for improving general ability will vary depending on the instructor and student, but might include concentrating on

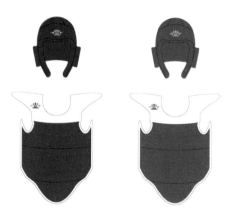

fluidity of kicks; aiming to hit with several fast kicks instead of one; stressing the need to return to a ready fighting position after executing a kick; and non-stop kicking speed drills. To improve accuracy, the student might try striking a tennis ball hanging from the ceiling, or kicking a dummy marked at key target points. Partners might wear such markers on their uniform during sparring.

GEAR

At the sport level, taekwondo is a well "protected" martial art. Although young students in most *dojang* require little more than their *dobok* and perhaps a t-shirt, an array of goods enhances the safety element of taekwondo in competition or sparring practice. Indeed players may more or less totally cover themselves in padded equipment if they so wish. Gloves help avoid knuckle and finger injury, whilst knee and elbow pads protect the joints. Given that the forearm can take a battering in the process of blocking, there are heavily padded forearm protectors specifically available to taekwondo practitioners. Large surfaces of the body can also be covered with chest, thigh, and shin protective gear, as the lower legs will often smash together at high speed. Mouth and groin guards are also used while the principle item of taekwondo equipment is a well-fitted helmet. Taekwondo shoes have been produced by some of the world's largest sports manufacturers and are available in a wide variety of designs. They should be tight, with a smooth surface conducive to repeated spinning, yet not too slippery and tough.

BELTS

New students are given a white belt to tie around the outside of the waist of their *dobok*, which it prevents from flapping open. The belt is first folded in half to find the midpoint, which is placed at the navel. The stripe side faces out while the tape end is on the right. Both sides are wrapped around the body to cross at the back and one is tucked under the other. The ends of the belt are then pulled down at the front to check that they are the same length on either side. The upper belt end is tucked under and then a loop is made through which one end is pulled. The ends are pulled tight to leave the stripe sides of both facing outward.

Belt colors may vary from *dojang* to *dojang*. Tags of the next color are applied to indicate near progression; for example, a green belt student might have a blue tag as the test for blue belt level approaches. Purple belts are also sometimes awarded, whilst some schools, reflecting the youthful make up of their student base, even have a "camo" (or camouflage) colored belt, which might be described as symbolically representing a sapling fighting its way through the taller pines.

MAKING THE GRADE

The student is periodically tested on basic moves, sparring, and forms as proficiency increases, starting out as a tenth degree (*geup*) novice at white belt before working down to first *geup* red and then advancing on to black belt status. At black belt level, the taekwondo student begins a new process of mastery and study, this time at first phase (*dan*). For the first three *dan* thereafter the student is once again referred to as a novice. The next three *dan* denote international instructor status, while seventh and eighth *dan* holders are simply called master. A fresh renewal point arrives at ninth *dan*, grand master, a status rarely conferred and achieved usually only by the sort of historical figures in the sport previously described in this book.

The *geup* and *dan* grades are narratively bound up in Korean history and tradition. For example, fourth *geup*, Jung-geun, is named after Ahn Jung-geun, an independence fighter of the early 20th century. Ahn mutilated his ring finger in a ritual pledge to fight the Japanese, and later assassinated the leader of a Japanese delegation to China, a senior administrator named Maquis Ito Hirobumi.

What might a student have to achieve to be awarded a fourth *geup*, Jung-geun, blue belt? Again, requirements may vary between schools, but typically might look like this. A minimum number of months in active training, including a set number of classes per week. Proficiency in numerous stances, such as rear foot, low, and close ready stance. Adeptness in particular kicks, such as the reverse turning kick, sweeping kick, jump turning kick, and a combination of consecutive kicks. Performance of the Jung-geun pattern, an elaborate choreographed multidirectional series of 32 movements that the examinee must confidently maneuver through, executing kicks, strikes, stances, and foot movements, all the while pitting the *teul* with loud expiration of *gi* to illustrate correct breathing. A

A taekwondo class in Afghanistan

demonstration of step sparring, including attack, defense, and counter; for example, a right middle punch followed by a left reverse knifehand block, concluding with a lead leg front kick and right reverse high elbow on the counter. A series of grabs followed up by debilitating kicks or punches. A demonstration of breaking, involving downward or twist kick and the inward knifehand strike. And participation in at least one tournament within a set time frame to be decided by the *dojang*. Theory testing involves questions about belt color meaning and a description of the moves and meaning of the Jung-geun pattern.

Belt awarding ceremonies vary from the planned to the casual. Generally speaking, the instructor will tie the new belt around the student's waist, sometimes having tied it and untied it from around his own in a gesture designed to symbolize the passing on of knowledge. It may occur in private or in front of the class, and might even be done as soon as the test is complete. Some instructors suggest a period away from the *dojang* after a particularly intense grading test, in which students can reflect on their progress and return to training with renewed vigor. A great fuss is not made of the awarding since such a ceremony might promote ego, a facet of the human makeup taekwondo seeks to control.

The most common criticism of taekwondo instructional centers by aficionados is that they are established not to inculcate a holistic mastery of their intricate art, but rather as "belt factories," opened with a view to persuading parents that their child can reach black belt status in the shortest possible time. The above brief perusal of fourth *geup* suggests that time is one of the most important qualities that ought to be available to the budding taekwondo student.

THE DOJANG

A silver Hyundai minibus pulls up outside an apartment block. Painted on each side is a cartoon tiger dressed in *dobok* adopting the basic ready position. The owner of the Hanjin Taekwondo School steps out and opens the side doors to the bus. "Annyong haseyo, taekwondo sabu-nim!" say three waiting students in greeting, before climbing up onto the back seats of the bus. The children are dressed in full *dobok* and the school's t-shirt and, being the first age group of the day, wear white, yellow, or recently acquired green belts. It is 3 p.m. and time for their daily taekwondo lesson.

The *dojang* is on the second floor of a commercial premises, sandwiched between a hair salon on the ground floor and an Internet cafe on the third. If you walk past the building between now and late evening, you will intermittently hear the sound of command shouts, such as "junbi" and "sabunimge" and the students' acknowledging yells.

There are thousands of such taekwondo schools across South Korea. From the megalopolis of downtown Seoul to any small provincial town, parents have the opportunity to send their children to after-school *dojang* from the ages of three to eighteen. The schools can be anywhere from 50 to 150 "pyeong" in size (one pyeong equals 3.3 square meters), and be either part of a nationwide franchise or a simple mom and pop operation.

Taekwondo schools in Korea take their place among a roster of after-school educational institutes, which include not just extra coaching in the basic subjects of math, science, and English, but traditional elements of

learning such as Chinese script and the age old board game *baduk*. But taekwondo *dojang* provide more than just an outlet for physical exercise and education in an ancient martial art; they serve as a character building rite of passage.

Chapter Six

THE FUTURE OF TAEKWONDO

In a 2013 interview, Choue Chung-won, president of the World Taekwondo Federation, spoke of radical changes he believed might benefit the sport. "For taekwondo to have staying power in the Olympics and reinvent itself as a spectator sport, it needs to make larger strides in its evolution into a combat sport." He then outlined a series of thoroughgoing proposals. He mooted the introduction of octagon or circular rings to provide judges with better views; a new point system to reward punches, which Choue feels have almost been eliminated from taekwondo at the competitive level. He even suggested casting off the traditional *dobok* in favor of popular sports outfits to promote a larger range of motions and reduce heat and moisture.

Before Choue's comments, Oh Kyoung-ho, chairman of South Korea's Chung Cheong University, which regularly used to host the World Taekwondo Festival, had proposed a fundamental alteration in the direction of taekwondo. Oh suggested that taekwondo change its emphasis from sport to cultural promotion and spiritual discipline. He also criticized the infrastructure of the aging Kukkiwon in Seoul. He then talked of the need to expand taekwondo's onus, into "character, mobile games, sports fashion, movies and tour programs," in other words to raise taekwondo's profile through diversifying content. Oh said, in reference to the 2004 Athens Olympics, "Korean people were excited when Moon Dae-sung won a gold medal with a brilliant roundhouse kick in the final. However, in my point of view, it is much more important and meaningful that he showed respect to his opponent and the judges before and after the game."

MUJU TAEKWONDO PARK

The contradictions in urging a purer, "character," and spiritual based taekwondo whilst revamping its sports aspect and rallying its market potential may seem problematic. But taekwondo has

Choue Chung-won,
President of the World Taekwondo Federation

1. Taekwondo Arena (outside) 2. Taekwondo Arena (inside) 3 & 4.The 5th World Youth Taekwondo Camp (Jul 2013)

conquered the world of martial arts as a result of its mutability, its power to transform itself. Oh's fears over infrastructure were then emphatically answered with the construction of Muju Taekwondo Park (TAEKWONDOWON), a global hub for taekwondo spread over two million square meters of land in the province of North Jeolla. Muju Taekwondo Park is a theme park, events hall, academic research portal, and advanced training center for taekwondo athletes from around the world. It is open to the public and serves as a global tourist destination for taekwondo. Features include a museum and a "taekwondo experience," which provides visitors with a high-tech taste of a martial art. Built in proximity to the nine valleys of Mt. Baegunsan, the park has spectacular views in eight directions. Six bridges link the various onsite centers, each

designed to reflect the levels of advancement through taekwondo. The design of a five thousand-seat taekwondo arena is derived from the three *taegeuk* elements drawn from Oriental philosophy: heaven, earth, and humanity, which serve to represent the fundamental spirit of taekwondo. Costing over half a billion US dollars, Muju Taekwondo Park is a clear statement of intent from taekwondo's world governing body that the sport must periodically reinvigorate itself to maintain and increase its 80 million-strong body of enthusiasts.

On the smaller matter of presentation and design, a female taekwondo uniform that clings to the body using Lycra fabrics was presented to the WTF Expansion Committee in Mexico in 2013. On a larger matter close to the hearts of the generation of pioneers who fought in their lifetime to take taekwondo from its infancy to full fledged Olympic competition, the IOC confirmed taekwondo's status as a full-medal sport for the 2020 Olympic program. Having introduced a new scoring system in London in 2012 to eliminate judging controversies, and with the global spread of golds among eight nations, taekwondo has demonstrated its merits as a fluid sport martial art.

PARA-TAEKWONDO

In 2009, a "special" taekwondo world championships took place in Baku, Azerbaijian. It was the first disabled taekwondo competition to take place at a global level. The success of the event in which 36 male and femal para-taekwondoists competed led to its expansion the following year, when double that number competed in St. Petersburg, Russia. The event is growing annually and forms the basis of the WTF's ultimate goal, which is to have the sport included in the Paralympics.

Taekwondo is a prime example of a highly physical sport that is not limited by physical boundaries. The formal practice of para-taekwondo is not as an adapted adjunct to the original sport. It is identical with Olympic taekwondo, using the same Daedo Protector and Scoring System (PSS), instant video replay, and international referees. The only difference is the exclusion of head attacks and shorter rounds. The deaf, visually impaired, amputees, and individuals with other upper body disabilities have access to organized taekwondo training and events on a global level.

The rapid evolution of para-taekwondo and its growing popularity are evidenced in the changing make up of world championship winners. France took the overall title in 2009 wheras Russia finished on top in 2013, taking four golds among thirteen medals overall.

Taekwondo organizers started work from 2006 to ensure that through participation, marketing, and member federations' involvement, taekwondo was at the forefront of global sports embracing all, regardless of disability, race, or gender. Shiela Radziewicz, a black belt holder from the United States was invited to the fourth World Youth Taekwondo Camp in Muju as a special lecturer. She was born without arms and knee cartilage, but went on to become the first female para-taekwondo competitor in taekwondo history to earn a black belt solely by kicking.

Shiela Radziewicz

THE FUTURE OF TAEKWONDO

But the future of taekwondo is in the hands of those who practice it, and those who propogate it through their involvement in its administration, research, and medical-scientific development. Individuals such as sports scientist Gabriel Fife, an assistant professor of athletics training based in South Korea, and many like him are working to guarantee taekwondo's continued success.

INTERVIEW WITH GABRIEL FIFE

WHAT IS YOUR TAEKWONDO STORY?

When I was about nine, I wanted to be a Teenage Mutant Ninja Turtle. My parents took me to a local dojang where I first began learning taekwondo. We moved to Portland, Oregon, a few months later and I continued taking lessons from a few schools. I ended up staying with my longtime coach Narayan Gurung, a 1992 Olympian from Nepal.

PLEASE TALK ABOUT YOUR SPECIAL INTEREST IN THE SPORT.

My academic background is athletic training: sports injury prevention, emergency management, rehabilitation, and treatment. While studying medical science, I became especially interested in head injuries in the sport. Taekwondo was identified as the most injurious sport during the London Olympic Games and the second most at the 2008 Games. Most of my recent work has been on the biomechanics of head injury. However, I've been interested in the epidemiology of taekwondo injuries for a long time. That's the topic of my upcoming dissertation.

WHAT, FOR YOU, IS THE CORE OF TAEKWONDO?

Community, hard work, respect for others, and family fun. The practice of martial arts embodies these characteristics. Taekwondo is a good model exemplifying these.

WHERE AND WHAT WAS YOUR BEST TAEKWONDO EXPERIENCE?
The 1999 US Open. I was injured (hamstring) just prior to the US Open. However I stuck with basic conditioning training and doing whatever I could to stay on top of my game. At the US Open, I went through a tough bracket that had a few logistical glitches requiring me to fight two semifinal matches. I ended up with the silver medal. From this experience, I learned about hard work and perseverance, all in the face of physical pain.

WHAT ABOUT THE PEOPLE YOU HAVE MET THROUGH TAEKWONDO?
I am especially grateful to my coach Narayan Gurung, who showed me what it is to work hard, follow your dreams, and make a difference in other peoples' lives.

HOW HAS TAEKWONDO CHANGED YOU?
Without taekwondo, I would not be where I am today. I became interested in sports performance and injury management, which lead me to study athletic training. As an assistant professor of athletic training in South Korea, the home of taekwondo, I am literally living a dream in a land where I can make a big impact on a sport that is still learning about standardized prevention and management of injuries at taekwondo events.

WHY IS TAEKWONDO SO GLOBALLY SUCCESSFUL?
It is most likely a reflection of the hard work ethic of the post-Korean War generation, who wanted to show the world the beauty of their culture and people. It has deep roots in Confucianism.

WHAT, IN YOUR OPINION, NEEDS TO CHANGE IN THE SPORT OR THE WORLD OF TAEKWONDO?

Attention must be paid to the high incidence of competition-related injuries. For example, taekwondo has four times the number of concussions reported in American football. Hopefully, governing bodies will pay more attention to this and make efforts to improve the safety of the sport. And hopefully, that is where I will play a part in the sport's future.

WHAT IS YOUR ADVICE TO NEWCOMERS TO TAEKWONDO?
Enjoy the community that a *dojang* has to offer and always seek to help others through the hand of taekwondo.

IN YOUR OPINION, WHAT DOES THE FUTURE HOLD FOR TAEKWONDO?
The sky's the limit. It has held its position on the Olympic podium since 200 and continues to make changes in competition rules in efforts to improve spectator appeal. With the support of the South Korean government, taekwondo will only continue to improve.

At the 17th World Taekwondo Federation General Assembly in Ho Chi Minh City, Vietnam, on July 25, 2006, the number of WTF member nations rose to 182. Within a few years, that total had surpassed 200 and the WTF was now on par with FIFA, the governing body of soccer, the world's most popular sport, for member countries. The growth of taekwondo has reached the point where it can only consolidate; few parts of the world have not been touched by taekwondo.

That consolidation is a job for Gabriel Fife's generation of practitioners to undertake. The guidance and adminstration of the pioneers, the grandmasters born in the first half of the twentieth century, is now in a passing phase. A video of an ITF international instructors course, taken in 2002, shows General Choi Hong-hi offering tips on correct execution of the Yong-gae *teul* to a sixth *dan* black-belt student. The video purports to be his last seminar, since he was, at age 83, in the grips of a decline that would see him pass away within months. Stories of the general were legion, of him stubbing cigarettes out on his own knuckles, of the thump thump of the seventy-year-old man conditioning his hands heard through hotel room walls, and of the patiently issued mantra "not like this, like this" as he demonstrated the correct block, stance or pattern. The man who had said he wished "to dwell in the world existing beyond the limits of time and space," was, in his ninth decade, while playfully tipping over a much younger black belt to the delight of the assembled masters, demonstrating that the process of taekwondo is serious, convivial, and elusive, and that the process never ends.

TAEKWONDO ROBOTS

The worlds of science and martial arts met in 2010, when robots programmed to detect, counter, and respond to taekwondo moves fought each other in a competition staged by the South Korean Knowledge Economy Ministry. This mix of the ancient and futuristic was administered under traditional rules: three rounds of three minutes each judged by three officials. The swift, complex, and repetitive movements demanded by taekwondo are ideal forms through which to test the anatomical modeling of mechanical robots, while at the same time offering a unique forum in which to promote the sport.

But the event was not a one off. In 2013, robots were slated to duke it out in the 12th Intelligent System-on-Chip (SoC) Robot War, hosted by the Korea Advanced Institute of Science and Technology (KAIST). Armed with a camera and semiconductor chips, each robot had 21 joints of humanoid correlation with which to attack and counter with front and side kicks and punches. The robots were developed by KAIST's System Design Innovation & Application Research Center in conjunction with the World Taekwondo Federation.

At this early stage of their development, the robots are not as skilled taekwondoists as their human creators, but their advent begs the question of whether there will one day be official sparring between taekwondo man and taekwondo machine. The Korea Taekwondo Association supplies its national team members with a series of training robots designed to push them to the limit . The machines incorporate a sophisticated online combat simulation program. Each one has a cybernetic system that measures speed, power, and reaction to each strike. They were designed to give competitors an aerobic and anaerobic edge in competition.

APPENDIX

INFORMATION

Further Information

TAEKWONDO ORGANIZATIONS

- TPF (Taekwondo Promotion Foundation)
  www.tpf.kr

- KTA (Korea Taekwondo Association)
  www.koreataekwondo.org/KTA_ENG

- Kukkiwon (World Taekwondo Headquarters)
  www.kukkiwon.or.kr

- WTF (World Taekwondo Federation)
  www.wtf.org/wtf_eng

- ITF (International Taekwondo Federation)
  www.itfline.org

- Olympic.org (Official website of the Olympic Movement)
  www.olympic.org/taekwondo

- World Taekwondo Peace Corps
  www.tpcorps.org/index_eng.html

2014 TAEKWONDO EVENTS

- WTF Qualification Tournament for Nanjing 2014 YouthOlympic Games
  (Mar 23–25, New Taipei City, ChineseTaipei)

- 10th WTF World Junior Taekwondo Championships
  (Mar 26–29, New Taipei, ChineseTaipei)

- 9th WTF world Taekwondo Poomsae Championships

- All African Games for Juniors (May, Botswana)

- 13th World University Taekwondo Championships
  (June 8–14, Hohhot, China)

- 2014 WTF World Grand-Prix Series 1 (July, TBD)

- Nanjing 2014 Youth Olympic Games (Aug 16–28, Nanjing, China)

- 2014 Oceania Taekwondo Championships

- 2014 Incheon Asian Game (Sep 19–Oct 4, Incheon, Korea)

- 2014 WTF World Grand-Prix Series 2 (Oct, TBD)

The content of this book has been compiled, edited, and supplemented from the following articles published in:

KOREANA, Vol. 4, No.3, Autumn 1990
"Yesterday's Korea Called Them 'Flowers of Youth'"
by Lee Jin-soo

KOREANA, Vol. 14, No. 4, Winter 2000
"Taekwondo's Philosophy and Aesthetics" by Lim Il-hyeok
"Traditional Korean Martial Arts Documented in
  Muyedobotongji" by Sim Woo-sung
"Taekgyeon" by Jeong Gyeong-hwa

PHOTOGRAPHS

Image Today 5, 8, 11, 27, 30
Kukkiwon 21, 46, 51, 65, 91, 93, 112
KTigers cover, 76, 77, 82
Korea Taekwondo Association (KTA) 41, 47
National Museum of Korea 20, 22
Taekwondo Promotion Foundation (TPF) 29, 34, 42, 45, 48, 50, 54, 57, 61, 62, 79, 94, 102, 103, 104
World Taekwondo Peace Corps 70, 71
Yonhap Photo 7, 12, 13, 15, 16, 17, 19, 21, 23, 24, 25, 28, 29, 33, 38, 39, 43, 46, 53, 58, 64, 66, 67, 69, 70, 72, 73, 75, 80, 84, 86, 88, 91, 93, 97, 99, 101, 103, 105, 108, 110, 111

CREDITS

Publisher   Kim Hyung-geun

Writer   NB Armstrong
Editor   Kim Hwa-pyeong
Copy Editor   D. Peter Kim

Designer   Cynthia Fernández